A POCKET GUIDE TO FINANCE

DAVID J. LEAHIGH, PH. D.
ASSISTANT PROFESSOR OF FINANCE
KING'S COLLEGE

THE DRYDEN PRESS
HARCOURT BRACE COLLEGE PUBLISHERS

FORT WORTH PHILADELPHIA SAN DIEGO NEW YORK ORLANDO AUSTIN SAN ANTONIO
TORONTO MONTREAL LONDON SYDNEY TOKYO

Address for Editorial Correspondence
The Dryden Press
301 Commerce Street, Suite 3700
Fort Worth, TX 76102

Address for Orders
The Dryden Press
6277 Sea Harbor Drive
Orlando, Florida 32887
1-800-782-4479, or 1-800-433-0001 (in Florida)

ISBN: 0-03-015718-8

Printed in the United States America

5 6 7 8 9 0 1 2 3 4   066   9 8 7 6 5 4 3 2 1

The Dryden Press Series List in Finance

Amling & Droms
Investment Fundamentals

Berry & Young
**Managing Investments: A Case
Approach**

Bertisch
Personal Finance

Brigham
**Fundamentals of Financial
Management**
Seventh Edition

Brigham
**Fundamentals of Financial
Management:
The Concise Edition**

Brigham, Gapenski, & Shome
**Cases in Financial Management:
The Dryden Request**

Brigham & Gapenski
**Cases in Financial Management:
Module A**

Brigham & Gapenski
**Cases in Financial Management:
Module B**

Brigham & Gapenski
**Cases in Financial Management:
Module C**

Brigham & Gapenski
**Financial Management: Theory
and Practice**
Seventh Edition

Brigham & Gapenski
**Intermediate Financial
Management**
Fifth Edition

Brigham, Aberwald, & Gapenski
Finance with Lotus 1-2-3
Second Edition

Chance
An Introduction to Derivatives
Third Edition

Clark, Gerlach, & Olson
**Restructuring Corporate
America**

Clauretie & Webb
**The Theory and Practice of Real
Estate Finance**

Cooley
**Advances in Business Financial
Management: A Collection of
Readings**
Second Edition

Cooley
**Business Financial
Management**
Third Edition

Dickerson, Campsey, & Brigham
**Introduction to Financial
Management**
Fourth Edition

Eaker, Fabozzi, & Grant
International Corporate Finance

Reilly & Norton
Investments
Fourth Edition

Siegel & Siegel
Futures Markets

Sears & Trennepohl
Investment Management

Smith & Spudeck
Interest Rates: Principles and Applications

Seitz & Ellison
Capital Budgeting and Long-Term Financing Decisions
Second Edition

Weston, Besley, & Brigham
Essentials of Managerial Finance
Eleventh Edition

The Harcourt Brace College Outline Series

Baker
Financial Management

INTRODUCTION

It has been my experience as a teacher of finance courses that students frequently need to find a definition or formula quickly. They don't want to spend a lot a time rereading a full sized textbook to find what they need. This book is designed to be a quick reference volume for students in upper division finance courses, particularly those in case courses. I have attempted to include as many of those formulas and concepts that are useful to such students, without incorporating the level of detailed explanatory material found in a standard introductory textbook. Thus the formulas should be easy to locate, either in the formulas section at the end of the text, or in the body of the text.

This Guide is not intended to be a textbook. There are many fine financial management texts on the market, and I do not want to compete with them. I have included a table that lists several of the current texts and the chapters in each in which the various topics are covered. The hope is that students will refer to the textbooks for a more detailed treatment of a particular topic presented here.

Being a first edition, there are, despite my best efforts, likely to be errors and omissions in the text. For these, I take full responsibility. I would be most grateful to have these mistakes pointed out, as well as for any suggestions - additions, deletions, and so on - on how to improve the Guide in the future.

I'd like to thank Edward J. Schoen, Dean of the William G. McGowan School of Business at King's College, for his encouragement and support of this project. I'd also like to thank Shana Lum of The Dryden Press for her enthusiasm for the project and for all her efforts to bring it to fruition. Paraphrasing Yogi Berra, I'd like to thank my students over the years for making this book necessary. If you'd kept your finance textbooks, I wouldn't have needed to write this one. And finally but by no means least, I'd like to thank my wife Maureen, without whom all of this wouldn't be nearly so much fun!

David J. Leahigh
King's College
Wilkes Barre, PA
August 1995

TABLE OF CONTENTS

CHAPTER 1
TIME VALUE OF MONEY

I. THE NATURE OF THE TIME VALUE OF MONEY
A. The *principle of the time value of money* states that a
dollar today is worth more than a dollar tomorrow.
B. It is important to note that this principle is independent of
changes in the general price level.

II. BASIC CONSIDERATIONS
A. Future Value vs. Present Value
1. *Future value* refers to the worth of an amount to be
received at some point beyond today.
2. *Present value* refers to the worth today of an amount that
will not be received or paid until some date in the future.
B. Nature of Cash Flows
1. A *lump sum* payment is a single cash flow.
2. An *annuity* is a series of cash flows of a fixed size that
occurs at regular intervals.
   a. An *ordinary annuity* is an annuity in which the
   payments are made at the <u>end</u> of the time period in
   question.
   b. An *annuity due* is an annuity in which the payments are
   made at the <u>beginning</u> of the time period in question.
   NOTE: A mortgage payment is usually an ordinary
   annuity, while rent is usually an annuity due.
C. The distinctions given above suggest that there are only
four basic time value problems. The following chart
summarizes these four problems, with reference to the
section of this chapter that deals with each:

	FUTURE VALUE	**PRESENT VALUE**
LUMP SUM	III.A	III.B
ANNUITY	IV.A	IV.B

1

D. Timing Conventions

It is assumed throughout this book that the present time or the current period is denoted as time zero (t_0). A payment made or received in one period from the present therefore occurs at time one (t_1), and so forth. This can be represented by the following time line:

```
|---------------|---------------|--------
```
t_0 t_1 t_2
(present)   (next   (two years
              year)   hence)

This convention simplifies computing the number of time periods involved.

E. Simple vs. Compound Interest

  1. *Simple interest* is a situation in which interest is computed only on the original principal.

  2. *Compound interest* is a situation in which interest is computed on the original principal and all previously accrued interest, that is, interest on interest. All the formulas in this chapter are based on compound interest.

F. Additivity of Cash Flows

A basic principle of time value is that the time values of a given type are <u>additive</u>. That is, the present values or future values of different forms of cash flows can be added together. For instance, one can find the present value of a lump sum and add it to the present value of an annuity to find the present value of the entire series of cash flows. This is a very useful concept in finding the value of an asset with compound cash flows or a project with uneven cash flows.

III. FUTURE VALUE

  A. The *future value of a lump sum* is given by the following equation:

$$FV_N = PV_0 * (1+r)^N \qquad (1.1)$$

where:

FV_N = future value at time N;

PV_0 = initial lump sum at time zero;

r = annual interest rate;

N = number of periods.

Equation 1.1 can also be written as:

$$FV_N = PV_0 * FVIF(r, N) \qquad (1.2)$$

where:

FVIF(r,N) = future value interest factor for r percent over N years and is equal to $(1 + r)^N$

Values for FVIF are given in Table A.1.

EXAMPLE: Find the future value at the end of 5 years of $1,000 invested today in an 8% deposit.

SOLUTION:

a. Using equation 1.1, we have:

$$FV_5 = \$1,000 * (1+.08)^5$$
$$= \$1,000 * 1.4693$$
$$= \underline{\$1,469.30}$$

b. Using equation 1.2 and Table A.1, we have:

$$FV_5 = \$1,000 * FVIF(8\%, 5)$$
$$= \$1,000 * 1.4693$$
$$= \underline{\$1,469.30}$$

B. The *future value of an ordinary annuity* is given by:

$$FVA_N = A * \frac{\left[(1+r)^N - 1\right]}{r} \tag{1.3}$$

where:
FVA_N = future value of an annuity at time N;
  A = ordinary annuity payment.

Using interest factors, this can be expressed as:

$$FVA_N = A * FVIFA(r, N) \tag{1.4}$$

where:
$FVIFA(r,N)$ = future value interest factor for an annuity for
  r percent and N periods and is equal to
$$\frac{\left[(1+r)^N - 1\right]}{r}$$

Values for FVIFA are given in Table A.3.

EXAMPLE: Find the future value of a $1,000 ordinary annuity over five years if the interest rate is 8%.
SOLUTION:
a. Using equation 1.3, we have:

$$FVA_5 = \$1,000 * \frac{\left[(1+.08)^5 - 1\right]}{.08}$$
$$= \$1,000 * \frac{1.4693 - 1}{.08}$$
$$= \$1,000 * 5.8666$$
$$= \$5,866.60$$

b. Using equation 1.4 and Table A.3, we have:

$$FVA_5 = \$1,000 * FVIFA(8\%, 5)$$
$$= \$1,000 * 5.8666$$
$$= \underline{\$5,866.60}$$

C. *The future value of an annuity due* is given by:

$$FVAD_N = A * \frac{\left[(1+r)^N - 1\right]}{r} * (1+r) \tag{1.5}$$

This is equivalent to:

$$FVAD_N = A * FVIFA(r, N) * (1+r) \tag{1.6}$$

EXAMPLE: Find the future value of a 5 year, $1,000 annuity due if the interest rate is 8%.
SOLUTION:
a. Using equation 1.5, we have:

$$FVAD_5 = \$1,000 * \frac{\left[(1+.08)^5 - 1\right]}{.08} * (1.08)$$

$$= \$1,000 * 5.8666 * 1.08$$

$$= \underline{\$6,335.93}$$

b. Using equation 1.6, we have:

$$FVAD_5 = \$1,000 * FVIFA(8\%, 5) * (1.08)$$

$$= \$1,000 * 5.8666 * 1.08$$

$$= \underline{\$6,335.93}$$

IV. PRESENT VALUE

A. *The present value of a lump sum* is given by:

$$PV_0 = \frac{FV_N}{(1+r)^N} \qquad (1.7)$$

Using interest factors, this is:

$$PV_0 = FV_N * PVIF(r,N) \qquad (1.8)$$

where:

PVIF(r,N) = present value interest factor for a lump sum at r percent for N years and is equal to

$$\frac{1}{(1+r)^N}$$

Values for PVIF are given in Table A.2.

EXAMPLE: Find the present value of a $5,000 payment due in 7 years, if interest rates are currently 9%.

SOLUTION:

a. Using equation 1.7, we have:

$$PV_0 = \frac{\$5,000}{(1+.09)^7}$$

$$= \frac{\$5,000}{1.8280}$$

$$= \$2,735.17$$

b. Using equation 1.8, and Table A.2, we have:

$$PV_0 = \$5,000 * PVIF(9\%,7)$$

$$= \$5,000 * .5470$$

$$= \$2,735.17$$

NOTE: Comparing equation 1.1 with 1.7 and equation 1.2. with 1.8 for present and future values of a lump sum, we see that they are the same basic equations.
Indeed, if we solve equation 1.2 for PV_0, we get:

$$PV_0 = \frac{FV_N}{FVIF(r,N)}$$

or:

$$PV_0 = FV_N * \frac{1}{FVIF(r,N)}$$

Comparing this to equation 1.8 we find that:

$$PVIF(r,N) = \frac{1}{FVIF(r,N)} \tag{1.9}$$

Thus, for lump sum problems, the two equations are the same. Just be careful in setting up the equation the proper way.
NOTE: This inverse relationship is <u>not</u> true for annuities.
B. The *present value of an ordinary annuity* is given by the following formula:

$$PVA_N = A * \frac{\left[1 - (1+r)^{-N}\right]}{r} \tag{1.10}$$

This is equivalent to:

$$PVA_0 = A * PVIFA(r,N) \tag{1.11}$$

Values for PVIFA are given in Table A.4.
EXAMPLE: Find the present value of a $5,000 ordinary annuity for 7 years if interest rates are 9%.

SOLUTION:
a. Using equation 1.10, we have:

$$PVA_N = \$5,000 * \frac{\left[1-(1+.09)^{-7}\right]}{.09}$$

$$= \$5,000 * \frac{1-.5470}{.09}$$

$$= \$5,000 * 5.033$$

$$= \underline{\$25,164.76}$$

b. Using equation 1.11 and Table A.4, we have:

$$PVA_0 = \$5,000 * PVIFA(9\%, 7)$$

$$= \$5,000 * 5.0330$$

$$= \underline{\$25,165.00}$$

The difference of 24 cents is due to the fact that a pocket calculator carries more digits than are given in tables.

C. The *present value of an annuity due* (PVAD) is given by the following formula:

$$PVAD = A * \frac{\left[1-(1+r)^{-N}\right]}{r} * (1+r) \qquad (1.12)$$

where:
PVAD = present value of an annuity due in N years.

This is equivalent to:

$$PVAD = A * PVIFA(r, N) * (1+r) \qquad (1.13)$$

EXAMPLE: Find the present value of $5,000 annuity due for 7 years if interest rates are 9%.
SOLUTION:
a. Using equation 1.12, we have:

$$PVAD = \$5,000*\frac{\left[1-(1+.09)^{-7}\right]}{.09}*(1.09)$$

$$= \$5,000*5.0330*(1.09)$$

$$= \underline{\$27,429.59}$$

b. Using equation 1.13 and table A.4, we have:

$$PVAD = \$5,000* PVIFA(9\%,7)*(1.09)$$

$$= \$5,000*5.0330*(1.09)$$

$$= \underline{\$27,429.85}$$

Again, the difference is due to rounding in the tables.
D. A *perpetuity* is an ordinary annuity that has an infinite series of equal payments.
The *present value of a perpetuity* is given by:

$$PVP = \frac{A}{r} \qquad\qquad (1.14)$$

where:
PVP = the present value of the perpetuity.

EXAMPLE: Find the present value of a perpetuity that pays $50 per year, if current interest rates are 8%.
SOLUTION: Using equation 1.14, we have:

$$PVP = \frac{\$50}{.08}$$

$$= \underline{\$625.00}$$

V. COMPOUNDING MORE THAN ONCE A YEAR

A. All the formulas given above assume interest is paid once a year. However, the payment of interest may occur more frequently than annually.

B. If compounding occurs more frequently than annually, it is necessary to modify the equations given above. For instance, equation 1.1 for the future value of a lump sum now becomes:

$$FV_N = PV_0 * \left(1 + \frac{r}{q}\right)^{N*q} \tag{1.15}$$

where:
q = number of times within a period compounding occurs.

Thus q = 2 for semi-annual compounding, q = 12 for monthly compounding, and q = 365 for daily compounding. In the alternative formula, we have:

$$FV_N = PV_0 * FVIF\left(\frac{r}{q}, N*q\right) \tag{1.16}$$

All the other equations above are modified in the same fashion: divide the annual interest rate by the number of compounding periods within a year, and multiply the number of years by the number of compounding periods.

EXAMPLE: Find the future value of a $1,000 deposit made today at 8%, if the deposit is held for 5 years and the interest is compounded daily.

SOLUTION: For daily compounding, q = 365. Using equation 1.16, we have:

$$FV = \$1,000 * \left(1 + \frac{.08}{365}\right)^{365*5}$$
$$= \$1,000 * (1 + .000219)^{1,825}$$

$$= \$1,000 * 1.491759$$
$$= \underline{\$1,491.76}$$

Compare this result with the example on page 3 for future value of a lump sum with annual compounding.

C. For _continuous compounding_, we must use:

$$FV_N = PV_0 * e^{r*N}$$
(1.17)

where:
e = base of the natural logarithm.

EXAMPLE: Find the future value of a $1,000 deposit made today for five years if interest rates are 8%, compounded continuously.
SOLUTION: Using equation 1.17, we have:

$$FV_N = \$1,000 * e^{.08*5}$$
$$= \$1,000 * 1.491825$$
$$= \underline{\$1,491.83}$$

Compare this with the example of daily compounding.

D. These examples serve to show a basic relationship: the more frequently compounding occurs, the greater the future value of any series of cash flows.
E. The _effective annual rate_ (EAR) is the annual interest rate equivalent to a given rate that has been compounded q times in a year. It is given by:

$$EAR = \left(1 + \frac{r_{nom}}{q}\right)^q - 1.0$$
(1.18)

where r_{nom} is the nominal annual rate.

11

EXAMPLE: Find the effective annual rate for a deposit that pays 8% annually, but compounded daily.
SOLUTION: Using equation 1.18:

$$EAR = \left(1 + \frac{.08}{365 - 1.0}\right)^{365} - 1.0$$

$$= (1.000219)^{365} - 1.0$$

$$= 1.083278 - 1.0$$

$$= .083278 \text{ or } \underline{8.3278\%}$$

VI. APPLICATIONS OF TIME VALUE CONCEPTS

   A. In all the applications above, we have solved for either a present or future value. There are several classes of problems that require solving for the cash flows, interest rates, or time periods. We consider some of the more typical ones here.

   B. Finding the Required Annuity

   1. To find the required annuity, use equation 1.10 (or 1.11) for present value or equation 1.3 (or 1.4) for future value, and then solve for A:

$$A = \frac{PVA_N}{PVIFA(r, N)} \tag{1.19}$$

$$A = \frac{FVA_N}{FVIFA(r, N)} \tag{1.20}$$

   2. The present value form is used in loan amortization problems, for instance. The future value form is used in accumulation problems.

   EXAMPLE: How much would you need to save each year in the form of an ordinary annuity in order to accumulate $50,000 in 6 years, if you could earn 7% a year?

SOLUTION: Use equation 1.20:

$$A = \frac{\$50,000}{FVIFA(7\%,6)}$$

$$= \frac{\$50,000}{7.1533} = \underline{\$6,989.79}$$

C. Loan Amortization

1. An *amortized loan* is one whose principal is paid back gradually over time. Most mortgages and car loans are amortized. To find the required payment and set up the amortization schedule, one first uses equation 1.19 to find the annuity A:

$$A = \frac{PVA_N}{PVIFA(r,N)}$$

2. The annuity A is the level amount necessary to repay principal and interest over the life of the loan. It includes both interest and principal, but the amount going to each changes from payment to payment. The amortization schedule is set based on the assumption that interest is charged only on the remaining principal balance.
   EXAMPLE: Set up an amortization schedule for a 4 year, $10,000 loan at 10%, if the payments are made yearly the end of the year.
   SOLUTION:
   a) Using equation 1.19, find the size of the level payment:

$$A = \frac{\$10,000}{PVIFA(10\%,4yrs)}$$

$$= \frac{\$10,000}{3.1699}$$

$$= \underline{\$3,154.67}$$

b) The interest component of the first payment is found by realizing that the borrower has the use of the full $10,000 for the entire first year. Therefore the interest component is:

$$Interest = .10 * \$10,000$$
$$= \$1,000$$

The principal component of the first payment is then the difference between the total payment and the interest component:

$$Principal\ Component = \$3,154.67 - \$1,000$$
$$= \$2,154.67$$

c) Set up the amortization schedule by using the fact that the outstanding principal balance has been reduced by $2,154.67:

TIME	BEGINNING BALANCE	INTEREST PAYMENT	PRINCIPAL PAYMENT	REMAINING BALANCE
1	$10,000.00	$1,000.00	$2,154.67	$7,845.33
2	$7,845.33	$784.53	$2,370.14	$5,475.19
3	$5,475.19	$547.52	$2,607.17	$2,868.02
4	$2,868.02	$286.80	$2,867.87	$0.15

The 15 cents left over is due to rounding.

D. Finding the Interest Rate or Number of Periods
   1. The equations above can also be used to find the interest rate, given the other parameters of the problem. This type of problem occurs in finding growth rates, for instance.
   EXAMPLE: Find the interest rate necessary to make $1,000 invested today grow to $1,593.85 in 8 years.
   SOLUTION: Use equation 1.1:

$$\$1,593.85 = \$1,000*(1+r)^8$$

$$1.5938 = (1+r)^8$$

$$r = (1.5938)^{\frac{1}{8}} - 1$$

$$r = .06 \text{ or } \underline{6\%}$$

You could also use equation 1.2 and Table A.1 by noting that 1.5938 is the FVIF for 8 years. Looking across the 8 year row in Table A.1, we find the value 1.5938 at 6%.

2. The above equations can also be used to find the number of periods, given the other parameters of the problem.
   EXAMPLE: How long will it take a $1,000 ordinary annuity at 5% to grow to $15, 917.13?
   SOLUTION: Use equation 1.4:

$$\$15,917.13 = \$1,000*FVIFA(5\%,N)$$

$$15.9171 = FVIFA(5\%,N)$$

Use Table A.3 and look down the 5% column. We find the value 15.9171 at 12 years.

NOTE: The *Rule of 72* is an approximation for finding either the interest rate or number of years necessary for a given lump sum to double. The rule states that the interest rate times the number of years is equal to 72. For example, to find out how long it will take for money to double at 9%, divide 9 into 72, to get 8 years. The actual answer is 8.04 years, but the rule does yield reasonable approximations.
E. Linear Interpolation
   1. Not all values for interest factors are tabled, just those for integral values of interest rates and periods. If the interest rate or number of periods sought is not an integer, then one can use *linear interpolation*. This method uses a straight line approximation to the true relationship.

2. Let the known interest factor be P' and its unknown parameter (time periods or interest rate) be Y'. Choose two pairs of interest factors and parameters (P_1, Y_1) and (P_2, Y_2) such that $P_1 < P' < P_2$. Then we know that Y' is between Y_1 and Y_2. Linear interpolation uses the following formula to obtain an approximation of Y':

$$Y' = \frac{(P' - P_1)}{(P_2 - P_1)}(Y_2 - Y_1) + Y_1 \qquad (1.21)$$

EXAMPLE: Suppose a person has deposited $1,000 in a bank for 10 years, and is promised $2,500 at the end of that time. What is the interest rate on the deposit?
SOLUTION: Find the interest factor:

$$2,500 = 1,000 * FVIF(Y', 10yrs.)$$

$$2.5 = FVIF$$

This factor lies between 9% (Y_1) and 10% (Y_2). The values for FVIF at these two rates are:

$$FVIF(9\%, 10yrs) = 2.3674$$
$$FVIF(10\%, 10yrs) = 2.5937$$

Now use equation 1.21:

$$Y' = \frac{2.5000 - 2.3674}{2.5937 - 2.3674} * (10\% - 9\%) + 9\%$$

$$= .5859(1\%) + 9\%$$

$$= \underline{9.5859\%}$$

The exact answer is 9.60%.
Interpolation works best when the distance between the two known parameters is not great.

CHAPTER 2
RISK AND RETURN

I. RISK AND RETURN
  A. _Return_ is the total increase or decrease in the value of an investment. It consists of the increase or decrease in the price of the investment plus the periodic payments, if any, made to the investor, such as interest or dividends.

  B. _Risk_ is the variability of returns from an investment.

  C. A fundamental principle of finance is that the greater the risk from an investment, the greater the expected return must be for the investor. The problem is then one of defining risk and expected return in a proper fashion.

II. RISK AND RETURN FOR A SINGLE ASSET
  A. Return Concepts

    1. The _holding period return_ (HPR) for a single asset is:

$$HPR = \frac{P_N - P_0}{P_0} + \frac{\sum_{t=1}^{N} CF_t}{P_0} \qquad (2.1)$$

where:
P_0 = original price;
P_N = final price;
CF_t = cash flow at time t;
N = length of investment.

For a single period, this becomes:

$$HPR = \frac{P_1 - P_0}{P_0} + \frac{CF_1}{P_0} \qquad (2.2)$$

These formulas can be used for realized returns and cash flows as well as expected returns and cash flows.

2. The *arithmetic average return* is defined by:

$$\overline{R} = \frac{\sum\limits_{t=1}^{N} HPR_t}{N} \tag{2.3}$$

$$= \frac{HPR_1 + HPR_2 + \ldots + HPR_N}{N} \tag{2.4}$$

where:
HPR_t = the holding period return for perod t.

3. The *geometric average return* is defined by:

$$\overline{G} = \left[\prod_{t=1}^{N} (1 + HPR_t) \right]^{\frac{1}{N}} - 1 \tag{2.5}$$

$$= \left[(1 + HPR_1)(1 + HPR_2)\ldots(1 + HPR_N) \right]^{\frac{1}{N}} - 1 \tag{2.6}$$

For simplicity from this point on, we will denote a holding period return as R_t.
NOTE: For a time series of returns on which compounding has occurred, the geometric average is preferable. However, measures of the dispersion of returns are based on the arithmetic average and thus is the more common.
EXAMPLE: Find the arithmetic and geometric averages for the following series of realized returns:
10%, 6%, -4%, 8%, 12%.
SOLUTION: The arithmetic mean is:

$$\overline{R} = \frac{\left[10\% + 6\% + (-4\%) + 8\% + 12\% \right]}{5}$$

$$= \frac{32\%}{5}$$
$$= \underline{6.40\%}$$

The geometric mean is:
$$G = \left[(1+.10)(1+.06)(1-.04)(1+.08)(1+.12)\right]^{1/5} - 1$$
$$= \left[1.3540\right]^{1/5} - 1$$
$$= .0625 \text{ or } \underline{6.25\%}$$

NOTE: The geometric average is always less than or equal to the arithmetic average.

4. The *expected return* is based on an explicit probability distribution of possible outcomes:

$$E(R) = \sum_{i=1}^{N} R_i * P(R_i) \tag{2.7}$$

$$= R_1 * P(R_1) + R_2 * P(R_2) + \ldots + R_N * P(R_N) \tag{2.8}$$

where:
$P(R_i)$ = the probability of the outcome R_i occurring.

B. Risk Concepts
1. The *variance* σ^2 of a series of realized returns is:

$$\sigma^2 = \frac{\sum_{t=1}^{N}(R_t - \overline{R})^2}{N-1} \tag{2.9}$$

$$= \frac{(R_1 - \overline{R})^2 + (R_2 - \overline{R})^2 + \ldots + (R_N - \overline{R})^2}{N-1} \tag{2.10}$$

The *standard deviation* σ is the square root of the variance:

$$\sigma = \sqrt{\sigma^2} \tag{2.11}$$

The *variance of an expected return* is:

$$\sigma^2 = \sum_{i=1}^{N} \left[R_i - E(R) \right]^2 * P(R_i) \tag{2.12}$$

$$= \left[R_1 - E(R) \right]^2 * P(R_1) + \left[R_2 - E(R) \right]^2 * P(R_2) + ...$$
$$+ \left[R_N - E(R) \right]^2 * P(R_N) \tag{2.13}$$

The *standard deviation for expected returns* is again the square root of the variance.

2. The *coefficient of variation* (CV) is a relative measure of risk, specifically, the risk per unit return. For realized returns, it is defined by:

$$CV = \frac{\sigma}{\overline{R}} \tag{2.14}$$

For expected returns, it is defined by:

$$CV = \frac{\sigma}{E(R)} \tag{2.15}$$

EXAMPLE: Find the variance, standard deviation, and the coefficient of variation for the following series: 10%, 6%, -4%, 8%, 12%.
SOLUTION: From a previous example we found the arithmetic average to be 6.40%. The variance is:

$$\sigma^2 = [(10-6.40)^2 + (6-6.40)^2 + (-4-6.40)^2 + (12-6.40)^2 + (8-6.40)^2]/(5-1)$$

$$= \frac{12.96+0.16+108.16+31.36+2.56}{4}$$

$$= \frac{155.2}{4} = \underline{38.8}$$

The standard deviation is:

$$\sigma = \sqrt{\sigma^2}$$

$$= \sqrt{38.8} = \underline{6.229\%}$$

The coefficient of variation is:

$$CV = \frac{\sigma}{\overline{R}}$$

$$= \frac{6.229}{6.40} = \underline{.973}$$

III. RISK AND RETURN FOR A PORTFOLIO
A. A *portfolio* is a set of individual securities.
B. Measures of Return
   1. The basic measure of return for a portfolio is the *expected return*:

$$E(R_p) = \sum_{i=1}^{N} \left[w_i E(R_i) \right] \tag{2.16}$$

$$= w_1 E(R_1) + w_2 E(R_2) + ... + w_N E(R_N) \tag{2.17}$$

where:

21

$E(R_i)$ = the expected return for security i;

w_i = the weight of the ith security in the portfolio, with $\Sigma w_i = 1$.

This is an *ex ante*, or before the fact, measure.

2. The *ex post*, or after the fact, or realized return of a portfolio is given by:

$$R_p = \sum_{i=1}^{N} w_i (R_i) \tag{2.18}$$

$$= w_1 R_1 + w_2 R_2 + ... w_N R_N \tag{2.19}$$

where:

R_i = realized return on security i.

The difference between the two equations is that the first one is based on <u>expected</u> future returns and the second is based on <u>actual</u> realized returns.

C. Measures of Portfolio Risk

1. The *covariance* COV_{XY} between two random variables measures the absolute comovement between the two. Mathematically it is given by:

$$Cov_{XY} = \frac{\sum_{i=1}^{N} (X_i - \overline{X})(Y_i - \overline{Y})}{N-1} \tag{2.20}$$

$$= \frac{(X_1 - \overline{X})(Y_1 - \overline{Y}) + (X_2 - \overline{X})(Y_2 - \overline{Y}) + ... + (X_N - \overline{X})(Y_N - \overline{Y})}{N-1}$$

2. The *correlation coefficient* ρ_{XY} between two random variables X and Y also measures the comovement between the two. Mathematically it is defined as:

$$\rho_{XY} = \frac{Cov_{XY}}{\sigma_X \sigma_Y} \tag{2.21}$$

The advantage of the correlation coefficient over covariance is that it does not depend on the scale of the two variables. The correlation coefficient is bounded between -1 and +1:

$$-1 \leq \rho_{XY} \leq +1$$

3. The *risk of a portfolio* is measured by its variance, which is given by the following formula:

$$\sigma_p^2 = \sum_{i=1}^{N} \sum_{j=1}^{N} \rho_{ij} w_i w_j \sigma_i \sigma_j \tag{2.22}$$

For a two security portfolio, this equation becomes:

$$\sigma_p^2 = w_1^2 \sigma_1^2 + w_2^2 \sigma_2^2 + \rho_{1,2} w_1 w_2 \sigma_1 \sigma_2 \tag{2.23}$$

where:
σ_p^2 = standard deviation of the portfolio;
w_i = weight of the ith security in the portfolio;
σ_i = standard deviation of the ith security;
$\rho_{1,2}$ = correlation coefficient between the two securities.

One could also use the standard deviation σ_p as a measure of the risk. The general formula is:

$$\sigma_p = \sqrt{\sum_{i=1}^{N} \sum_{j=1}^{N} \rho_{ij} w_i w_j \sigma_i \sigma_j} \tag{2.24}$$

The two security case is:

$$\sigma_p = \sqrt{w_1^2 \sigma_1^2 + w_2^2 \sigma_2^2 + 2\rho_{1,2} w_1 w_2 \sigma_1 \sigma_2} \tag{2.25}$$

NOTE: The standard deviation of the return of a portfolio is not a linear function of the standard deviations of the individual securities held in the portfolio. The portfolio standard deviation depends critically on the correlation of the securities with one another. As the correlation declines, so does the risk of the portfolio. The risk associated with a portfolio's return can be reduced by choosing securities that are not highly correlated with each other.

D. A portfolio is said to be *efficient* if it maximizes expected return for a given level of risk, or minimizes risk for a given level of return.

EXAMPLE: Find the return, standard deviation, and variance of a portfolio with the following parameters:

$R_A = 10\%$ $\quad\quad$ $\sigma_1 = 15\%$ $\quad$ $w_1 = 40\%$

$R_B = 14\%$ $\quad\quad$ $\sigma_2 = 20\%$ $\quad$ $w_2 = 60\%$ $\quad$ $\rho_{A,B} = .5$

SOLUTION: Using equation 2.19, we find the return:

$$R_p = .4*10\% + .6*14\%$$
$$= 4\% + 8.4\%$$
$$= \underline{12.4\%}$$

The variance is found using equation 2.23:

$$\sigma^2 = (.4)^2(.15)^2 + (.6)^2(.20)^2 + 2(.2)(.4)(.6)(.15)(.20)$$
$$= .0036 + .0144 + .0029$$
$$= \underline{.0209}$$

The standard deviation is:

$$\sigma = \sqrt{.0209} = .1446 \text{ or } \underline{14.46\%}$$

The coefficient of variation is:

$$COV = \frac{.1446}{.124} = \underline{1.1661}$$

IV. THE CAPITAL ASSET PRICING MODEL

  A. The _Capital Asset Pricing Model_ (CAPM) is a model of the pricing of risk of assets. It is derived from the basic model of portfolio selection given above, with a couple of additional assumptions.

  B. Assumptions of the CAPM

    1. All investors choose their portfolios on the basis of risk and return.

    2. All investors can borrow and lend at a risk free rate of interest R_F.

    3. There are no transactions costs.

    4. All investors have the same expectations.

    5. All investors are risk averse.

  C. Capital Market Line

    1. Under the above assumptions, it can be shown that all investors will choose to hold all risky assets in proportion to the assets' market values. In other words, all investors hold the _market portfolio M_.

    2. The only other asset in the portfolio is the risk free asset. Positive amounts of the risk-free asset represent lending, and negative amounts represent borrowing.

    3. The _Capital Market Line_ (CML) is the risk-return tradeoff for efficient portfolios:

$$E\left(R_p\right) = R_F + \sigma_p \left[\frac{E\left(R_M\right) - R_F}{\sigma_M}\right] \tag{2.26}$$

where:

    R_F = the risk-free rate;

    σ_p = the risk on the portfolio;

  $E(R_M)$ = the expected return on the market portfolio;

    σ_M = the risk on the market portfolio.

  D. Security Market Line

    1. The _Security Market Line_ (SML) is the risk-return tradeoff for all portfolios, efficient and inefficient:

$$E(R_i) = R_F + \beta_i \left[E(R_M) - R_F \right] \tag{2.27}$$

where:

β_i = the *beta* of security i, defined below.

NOTE: All portfolios that are on the CML are on the SML as well. The converse is not true.

2. The coefficient β_i is called *beta* and is defined as:

$$\beta_i = \frac{Cov_{i,M}}{\sigma_M^2} \tag{2.28}$$

$$= \frac{\rho_{i,M} \sigma_i \sigma_M}{\sigma_M^2} \tag{2.29}$$

$$= \frac{\rho_{i,M} \sigma_i}{\sigma_M} \tag{2.30}$$

NOTE: Equations 2.28, 2.29, and 2.30 are equivalent. The choice of which one to use depends on the available parameters.

3. The beta of a security is a measure of its *market*, or *systematic*, or *non-diversifiable* risk. It has the following ranges:

   a. If $\beta = 1$, then the security or portfolio has the same amount of market risk as the market portfolio, and therefore requires the market return.

   b. If $\beta > 1$, then the security has more market risk than the market portfolio and requires more than the market return.

   c. If $0 < \beta < 1$, the security has less market risk than the market portfolio, and therefore requires a return less than the market.

   d. If $\beta < 0$, then the security is negatively correlated with the market portfolio, and on its own should earn less than the risk free rate.

NOTE: Beta is a measure of the risk a security brings to a well-diversified portfolio. It is different from the security's total risk. According to the SML, an investor is compensated only for taking on systematic risk.

EXAMPLE: Find the beta for the following two securities:

$$\rho_{1M} = .9 \qquad \sigma_1 = .20$$
$$\rho_{2M} = .5 \qquad \sigma_2 = .35$$
$$\sigma_M = .25$$

SOLUTION: Using equation 2.30, we have:

$$\beta_1 = \frac{.9*.20}{.25} = .72$$

$$\beta_2 = \frac{.5*.35}{.25} = .70$$

Note that security 1, while having a smaller standard deviation than security 2, has slightly more market risk. Therefore, security 1 would have a slightly higher required return.

4. A security's *total risk*, as measured by its variance, is given by:

$$\sigma_i^2 = \beta_i^2 \sigma_M^2 + \sigma_{ei}^2 \tag{2.31}$$

where:

σ_{ei}^2 = variance of security i's random residual error return.

The second term on the right hand side is a measure of the security's *specific*, or *unsystematic*, or *diversifiable* risk. It is the risk that can be elimated through proper diversification.

5. The *beta of a portfolio* β_P is the weighted average of the betas of the securities in a portfolio:

$$\beta_p = \sum_{i=1}^{N} w_i \beta_i \tag{2.32}$$

$$= w_1 \beta_1 + w_2 \beta_2 + ... + w_N \beta_N \tag{2.33}$$

E. Advantages and disadvantages of CAPM
1. Adavantages include:
   a. The model is relatively simple.
   b. It emphasizes the idea that not all risk is relevant in pricing securities.
2. Disadvantages include:
   a. The market is assumed to be the only source of relevant risk.
   b. The true market portfolio cannot be measured in practice. One can only measure the parameters for a proxy for the market portfolio.
F. Other models such as the arbitrage pricing theory address some of the problems of the CAPM. For a more detailed discussion of CAPM and its problems, please see Reilly, *Investment Analysis and Portfolio Management*, 4th edition, Chapter 25. (Fort Worth: Dryden Press, 1994.)

CHAPTER 3
VALUATION

I. WHAT IS A SECURITY WORTH?

A. _The value of a security_ V_S is the present value of expected future cash flows. Mathematically, this is:

$$V_S = \sum_{t=1}^{N} \frac{CF_t}{(1+k)^t}$$
$$= \frac{CF_1}{(1+k)} + \frac{CF_2}{(1+k)^2} + \ldots + \frac{CF_N}{(1+k)^N}$$

(3.1)

where:
V_S = value of a security;
CF_t = cash flow at time t;
k = the appropriate discount rate.

B. Most basic securities can be valued by this process. It will not work for more complex securities, such as options.

C. The value of a security is not necessarily its current market price. Please see Sections V. and VI. of this chapter for a discussion of this.

II. VALUATION OF BONDS

A. A _bond_ is a long term debt instrument with a maturity greater than one year that promises to pay periodic coupon interest I_t and a lump sum principal amount M at maturity N years from the present. The dollar amount of the coupon paid, I_t, is equal to the coupon rate times the principal value of the bond. Please see Chapter 9 for more on the institutional features of bonds.

NOTE: The coupon rate is fixed for the vast majority of bonds. The coupon rate should not be confused with the market rate of interest or yield to maturity, which is used to discount the cash flows.

B. Value of a Bond
  1. If coupons are paid annually, then the value of a bond
     V_B is given by:

$$V_B = \sum_{t=1}^{N} \frac{I_t}{(1+k_b)^t} + \frac{M}{(1+k_b)^N}$$

(3.2)

where:
  I_t = dollar coupon paid at time t;
  M = principal amount paid at time N;
  k_b = pre-tax yield for the bond.

This is equivalent to the following:

$$V_B = I_t * PVIFA(k_b, N) + M * PVIF(k_b, N)$$

(3.3)

  2. If coupons are paid <u>semi-annually</u>, then you must
     modify equations 3.2 and 3.3 by doing the following:
     a. <u>double</u> the number of payment periods;
     b. <u>divide</u> the required rate k_b by 2;
     c. <u>divide</u> the annual coupon payment by 2.
     Do <u>not</u> change the principal payment.
     The equations then become:

$$V_B = \sum_{t=1}^{2N} \frac{\dfrac{I_t}{2}}{\left(1+\dfrac{k_b}{2}\right)^t} + \frac{M}{\left(1+\dfrac{k_b}{2}\right)^{2N}}$$

(3.4)

and

$$V_B = \left(\frac{I_t}{2}\right) * PVIFA\left(\frac{k_b}{2}, 2N\right) + M * PVIF\left(\frac{k_b}{2}, 2N\right)$$

(3.5)

EXAMPLE: A 20 year, $1,000 par value bond has a 10% coupon and an 8% yield to maturity. Find the value of the bond if:
a) the coupon is paid annually;
b) the coupon is paid semi-annually.
SOLUTION:
a) The bond pays $100 annually. Using equation 3.3,

$$V = \$100 * PVIFA(8\%, 20) + \$1,000 * PVIF(8\%, 20)$$
$$= \$100 * 9.8181 + \$1,000 * .2145$$
$$= \underline{\$1,196.31}$$

b) The bond pays $50 every six months. There are 40 payment periods, and the semi-annual yield is 8%/2, or 4%. Using equation 3.5, the problem now is:

$$V = \$50 * PVIFA(4\%, 40) + \$1,000 * PVIF(4\%, 40)$$
$$= \$50 * 19.7928 + \$1,000 * .2083$$
$$= \underline{\$1,197.94}$$

NOTE: The answers for annual and semi-annual compounding are not identical.

3. A *zero coupon bond* is one that pays only a lump sum principal payment at maturity. Its value is given by:

$$V_B = M * \left(\frac{1}{1 + \dfrac{k_b}{2}} \right)^{2N} \tag{3.6}$$

This is the same as:

$$V_B = M * PVIF\left(\frac{k_b}{2}, 2N \right) \tag{3.7}$$

NOTE: Even though it pays no interest, a zero coupon bond is valued assuming semi-annual compounding.

C. Bond Yield Concepts

1. The *coupon rate* is the stated percent of par value that will be paid annually as interest.

2. The *current yield* (CY) equals the dollar coupon divided by the current market price of the bond:

$$CY = \frac{I_t}{P_0} \tag{3.8}$$

3. The *yield to maturity* (YTM) is that discount rate which sets the present value of all remaining future cash flows until the contract maturity equals the current price. It is the same thing as a bond's internal rate of return. You solve the following equation for YTM:

$$P_0 = \sum_{t=1}^{N} \frac{I_t}{(1+YTM)^t} + \frac{M}{(1+YTM)^N} \tag{3.9}$$

where YTM is the yield to maturity. This can also be expressed as:

$$P_0 = I_t * PVIFA(YTM, N) + M * PVIF(YTM, N)$$

$$\tag{3.10}$$

An *approximate yield to maturity* (AYTM) can be found using the following:

$$AYTM = \frac{I_t + \dfrac{(M - P_0)}{N}}{\dfrac{P_0 + M}{2}} \tag{3.11}$$

4. The *yield to call* (YTC) is that discount rate which sets the present value of all cash flows remaining until the first date that the bond can be called equal to the bond's current market price. The yield to call is similar to the yield to maturity except that only those coupon payments on or before the call date are considered, and the par value is replaced by call price, which is usually higher than par. One solves the following for YTC:

$$P_0 = \sum_{t=1}^{C} \frac{I_t}{(1+YTC)^t} + \frac{CP_c}{(1+YTC)^C} \tag{3.12}$$

where:
YTC = yield to call;
CP_c = call price;
C = time to earliest call date.

An *approximate yield to call* (AYTC) is given by:

$$AYTC = \frac{I_t + \dfrac{CP_c - P_0}{C}}{\dfrac{CP_c + P_0}{2}} \tag{3.13}$$

5. The *realized, or annual, rate of return* (ARR), is an ex-post ("after the fact") measure of return. It is calculated by first finding the *terminal value* (TV_N) of the bond. This is the total of all cash inflows resulting from the investment, including reinvestment income. This is then used in the following equation:

$$TV_N = PV_0 * (1 + ARR)^N \tag{3.14}$$

where:
PV_0 = the original amount invested;
N = number of periods the investment was held.

Solving for ARR:

$$ARR = \left(\frac{TV_N}{PV_0}\right)^{\frac{1}{N}} - 1 \tag{3.15}$$

This is simply an application of the future value of a lump sum formula, equation 1.1.

D. Price-Yield Relationships for Bonds
1. The current market price of a bond P_0 will in general be different from its par value M.
   a. If the market price does equal P_0, the bond is *trading at par*, and the coupon rate equals the yield to maturity.
   b. If the market price P_0 is less than its par value M, then the bond is trading *at a discount* and the yield to maturity is greater than the coupon rate.
   c. If the market price P_0 is greater than its par value M, then it is trading *at a premium* and the yield to maturity is less than the coupon rate.
2. The current market price P_0 of a bond and its yield to maturity YTM are inversely related.
3. The longer the time to maturity, the greater percentage change in the price of a bond for a given change in yield to maturity.

EXAMPLE: Find the coupon rate, current yield, the yield to maturity, and the yield to call for a bond that has $1,000 par value, pays $100 in interest annually, matures in 20 years, and is callable in 5 years at $1,100. The current price is $1091.25. Assume interest is paid annually.

SOLUTION:
a. The coupon rate is the annual interest divided by the principal, or 10%.
b. The current yield is found using equation 3.8:

$$CY = \frac{\$100}{\$1,091.25}$$

$$=.0916 \text{ or } \underline{9.16\%}$$

c. The yield to maturity is found by first noting that, because the bond is trading at a premium, the yield to maturity must be less than the 10% coupon rate. Trying 9% as a first guess, we find:

$$\$100*PVIFA(9\%,20) + \$1,000*PVIF(YTM,20) =$$

$$\$100*9.1285 + \$1,000*.1784$$

$$= \underline{\$1,091.25}$$

Because this is equal to the price, 9% is the yield to maturity.

d. The yield to call can be found in the same manner as the yield to maturity, changing the relevant parameters. You can also use the formula for the approximate yield to call, equation 3.13:

$$AYTC = \frac{\$100 + \dfrac{\$1,100 - \$1,091.25}{5}}{\dfrac{\$1,100 + \$1,091.25}{2}}$$

$$=.0929 \text{ or } 9.29\%$$

The actual YTC is 9.27%.

III. VALUATION OF PREFERRED STOCK

A. *Preferred stock* is a form of equity. It is separate from common equity in that holders of preferred stock have a priority of claim on income and on assets in the event of liquidation. It usually pays a fixed dividend D_p every period. Please see Chapter 9 for more information on preferred stock.

B. *Perpetual preferred stock* has no maturity date. Its value V_P is found by using the formula for a perpetuity, equation 1.14:

$$V_P = \frac{D_P}{k_P}$$ (3.16)

where:
D_P = the periodic (annual) preferred dividend;
k_P = the discount rate or required return on preferred.

EXAMPLE: Find the value of an issue of perpetual preferred stock that pays a $7 dividend if the required return is 12%.
SOLUTION: Using equation 3.16, we get:

$$V_P = \frac{\$7}{.12} = \underline{\$58.33}$$

C. *Limited life preferred stock* has a specified finite maturity date. It can be valued in the same manner as a bond, using equation 3.2 or one of the others, depending on the frequency of the dividend payment. The dividends take the place of the interest payments, and the par value replaces the principal of the bond.

IV. VALUATION OF COMMON STOCK

A. *Common stock* represents the residual ownership of the firm. Owners of common stock, or equity, are entitled to any earnings left over after everyone else has been paid. Again, please see Chapter 9 for more details on common stock.

B. The *value of common stock* V_E is given by the present value of expected future cash flows. In this case, however, the expected cash flows of common stock, namely dividends and proceeds from the sale of stock, are less certain than those for bonds and preferred stock. The value of common stock is found by:

$$V_E = \sum_{t=1}^{N} \frac{D_t}{(1+k_e)^t} + \frac{E(P_N)}{(1+k_e)^N} \qquad (3.17)$$

where:
D_t = dividend expected at time t;
$E(P_t)$ = expected market price at time N;
k_e = discount rate or required return for common equity.

C. Valuation of Common Equity: Specific Cases
  1. *Finite horizon:* use equation 3.17 above.
  2. The *constant growth model* assumes that the dividend will grow at a constant percentage $g < k_e$ for the indefinite future. Equation 3.16 is then equivalent to:

$$V_E = \frac{D_1}{k_e - g} = \frac{D_0(1+g)}{k_e - g} \qquad (3.18)$$

where:
D_1 = the expected dividend at period 1;
D_0 = the most recently paid dividend;
g = the expected constant growth rate.

EXAMPLE: Find the value of a stock that just paid a $1.00 dividend, has a growth rate of 6%, and has a required return of 10%.
SOLUTION: Using equation 3.18, we have:

$$V_E = \frac{(\$1.00)(1.06)}{.10-.06}$$
$$= \frac{\$1.06}{.04}$$
$$= \underline{\$26.50}$$

NOTE: Required returns and growth rates must be expressed in <u>decimal</u> form, not percentage form. The above formula also strictly requires that k_e be greater than g. Otherwise, absurd answers such as negative values will result.

NOTE: The assumption of constant growth over an infinitely long horizon is clearly just a mathematical simplification. Indeed, many studies have shown that growth, especially earnings growth, tends to be highly variable, even over short time horizons.

3. *Supernormal growth* is a situation in which the projected growth of the firm is temporarily greater than the required return for some finite period of time. In this case, formula 3.18 is invalid and the following must be used:

$$V_E = \sum_{t=1}^{N} \frac{D_t}{(1+k_e)^t} + \frac{D_{N+1}}{k_e - g}\left(\frac{1}{1+k_e}\right)^N \tag{3.19}$$

The first term on the right hand side is the present value of the dividends during super normal growth. The first part of the second term is the value at time N of all dividends after the period of supernormal growth. The second part of the second term simply discounts that value at time N back to the present.

EXAMPLE: Find the value of common stock of a company that just paid a $1.50 dividend. The dividend is expected to grow at 15% a year for the next 5 years, and then grow at 5% per year for the indefinite future. The required return is 10% for all time periods.

SOLUTION: First, find the dividends for the next six periods, D_1 through D_6:

$$D_1 = D_0 * (1 + g_1) = \$1.50*1.15 = \$1.73$$
$$D_2 = D_0 * (1 + g_1)^2 = \$1.50* (1.15)^2 = \$1.98$$
$$D_3 = D_0 * (1 + g_1)^3 = \$1.50* (1.15)^3 = \$2.28$$
$$D_4 = D_0 * (1 + g_1)^4 = \$1.50* (1.15)^4 = \$2.62$$
$$D_5 = D_0 * (1 + g_1)^5 = \$1.50* (1.15)^5 = \$3.02$$
$$D_6 = D_0 * (1 + g_1)^5 (1 + g_2) = \$1.50* (1.15)^5 (1.05) = \$3.17$$

Now use equation 3.19:

$$V = \frac{1.73}{(1.10)} + \frac{1.98}{(1.10)^2} + \frac{2.28}{(1.10)^3} +$$

$$+ \frac{2.62}{(1.10)^4} + \frac{3.02}{(1.10)^5} + \frac{3.17}{(.10-.05)} * \left(\frac{1}{(1.10)^5} \right)$$

$$= \$1.5727 + \$1.6364 + \$1.7130 + \$1.7895 +$$
$$+ \$1.8752 + \frac{\$63.40}{(1.10)^5}$$
$$= \$8.5868 + \$39.3664$$
$$= \underline{\$47.9532}$$

E. Estimation of the Parameters

1. The dividend for next period D_1 will depend on a number of factors, including the firm's traditional dividend policy, expected growth, legal restrictions, and so on. Many firms choose to maintain a constant dollar dividend, raising it only when earnings will support a permanent increase. Please see Chapter 8 for a more detailed treatment of dividend policy.
2. The *required return* k_e can be estimated in several ways:
   a. You can use equation 3.18 with the current market price P_0 to find k_e. This assumes that the stock price is its equilibrium price. This approach is used in

Chapter 4 in the context of estimating the cost of capital for the firm.

b. You can use the *Capital Asset Pricing Model* (CAPM), and specifically the *Security Market Line* (SML, equation 2.27) to estimate k_e:

$$k_e = R_f + \beta\left(R_M - R_f\right)$$

c. Finally, you can use *the bond plus risk premium* approach. This method involves finding the spread of the average stock return over the bond issue return, and then taking that spread and adding it to the particular firm's pre-tax cost of debt. The average stock has a beta of one, so its return is in essence the market return. Thus you take the market return minus the yield on the average (typically single A rated) bond. This is then added to the company's cost of debt to get k_e.

3. The *sustainable growth rate*, g, can be found by the following:

$$g = b * ROE \tag{3.20}$$

where:
   b = the retention ratio, which is equal to
      (Net Income - Dividends)/Net Income;
ROE = return on equity.

The retention ratio is also equal to one minus the dividend payout ratio.

a. If the sustainable growth rate is higher, then the retention ratio and the firm's ROE are higher.

b. Thus, the higher the firm's payout ratio, the lower the firm's level of sustainable growth.

NOTE: One of the most common mistakes made in estimating the value of common stock is to start with some idea of what the stock ought to be worth, and then deriving the parameter estimates to be consistent with that value. This is exactly the opposite of how it should be done.

V. VALUES AND PRICES
A. The above procedures develop the value V of the respective securities. This value can in theory be different from the current market price P.
B. In order to choose investments, you should use the following investment rules:
1. If the estimated value is greater than the current market price, then buy the security.
2. If the estimated value is less than the current market price, then sell the security short.

VI. EFFICIENT MARKETS AND VALUATION
A. A market for a security is said to be *efficient* if the security's current price reflects all available information.
B. There are three versions of the *Efficient Markets Hypothesis* (EMH):
1. *Weak form*: the current price reflects all historical price and market information.
2. *Semi-strong form*: the current price reflects all publicly available information.
3. *Strong form*: the current price reflects all information, both public and private.
C. Implications of EMH
1. In general, the EMH means that is not possible to derive a trading rule based on the particular set of information that would allow the investor to consistently earn positive, risk-adjusted excess returns. Value will on average be equal to price.
NOTE: In English, this really means, "You can't beat the market."
2. If the weak form EMH is true, then someone using historical price and volume data as the basis for a trading

rule would not earn excess risk-adjusted returns. Thus technical analysis would not be useful.

3. If the semi-strong version is true, then one could not use any public information and earn excess returns. This means that fundamental analysis of a security would not be useful.

4. If the strong form is true, then no set of information, public or private, could be used to earn excess returns. Therefore even insiders wouldn't be able to use such privileged information to make excess returns.

D. If the EMH is correct, then the value of a security will on average equal its price. Securities would be neither over- nor under-valued in any consistent, predictable fashion. Thus the best investment strategy would to buy and hold the market portfolio.

E. Evidence offers good support for the weak form, moderate support for the semi-strong form, and little support for the strong form.

CHAPTER 4
COST OF CAPITAL

I. THE COST OF CAPITAL
A. Definition and Assumptions
1. The *cost of capital* to a firm is the percentage cost of obtaining the next increment of long term financing.
2. It is typically assumed that new capital will be raised in the same proportions as are currently used by the firm on its balance sheet. These proportions are properly determined by using <u>market values</u> for the sources of capital, not book values.
3. The relationship between the cost of capital and changes in the capital structure is considered in Chapter 6.
B. The general procedure to find the cost of capital is as follows:
1. Estimate the component costs of capital for each available source of long term financing.
2. Estimate the market value based weights of each source of long term financing.
3. Calculate the weighted average cost of capital.
4. Calculate where "break points" will occur, that is, determine at what levels of financing the company will exhaust a lower cost source of funds and will be forced to use a higher cost source.
5. Calculate the weighted average cost of capital for the new, higher cost combination of funds.

II. ESTIMATING COMPONENT COSTS OF CAPITAL
A. The *cost of debt* k_d for a firm is the <u>after tax</u> cost of issuing new debt. This is because the interest cost is typically deductible for tax purposes. This is given by:

$$k_d = k_b(1-T) \qquad (4.1)$$

where:
k_b = pre-tax cost of issuing new debt;
T = the firm's marginal tax rate.

The pre-tax cost of debt k_b can be found using the methods in Chapter 3 for finding the yield to maturity.

EXAMPLE: Calculate the cost of new debt for a firm that currently has 20-year bonds outstanding with a 10% coupon paid annually and that are currently trading in the market at $1,091. The firm is in the 40% tax bracket.

SOLUTION: We must find the yield to maturity of the outstanding bonds:

$$\$1,091 = \$100 * PVIFA(YTM,20) + \$1,000 * PVIF(YTM,20)$$

Because the bond is trading at a premium, try an interest rate lower than the coupon rate, say 9%:

$$\$100 * 9.1285 + \$1,000 * .1784 = \underline{\$1,091}$$

In this case, the yield to maturity is exactly 9%. The after-tax cost of new debt is therefore:

$$k_d = 9.00\% * (1-.40)$$

$$= \underline{5.40\%}$$

B. The *cost of perpetual preferred stock* k_p is found by using equation 3.15, substituting P_p for V_p, modifying it for flotation costs, and solving for k_p:

$$k_p = \frac{D_p}{P_p - F} \qquad (4.2)$$

or

$$k_P = \frac{D_P}{P_P(1-f)} \tag{4.3}$$

where:

k_p = cost of preferred stock;
D_p = dividend on preferred;
P_p = issue price of preferred;
F = flotation costs in dollars associated with issuance;
f = flotation costs as a fraction of the issue price.

EXAMPLE: Find the cost of new preferred stock for a company if the new issue will pay a $7 annual dividend, will be sold to the public at $77 a share, and will cost the firm $5 per share in flotation costs, netting the firm $72 a share.
SOLUTION: Using equation 4.2, we have:

$$k_p = \frac{\$7}{\$77 - \$5}$$

$$= .0972 \text{ or } \underline{9.72\%}$$

C. Cost of Common Equity
    1. The *cost of common equity* in the form of *retained earnings* k_s can be estimated by several methods:
        a. Assuming constant growth, you can use equation 3.18, substituting P_0 for V, and solve for k_s:

$$k_s = \frac{D_1}{P_0} + g \tag{4.4}$$

where:

k_s = cost of capital for common equity;
D_1 = dividend expected next year;
P_0 = current market price;
g = growth rate.

NOTE: Raising equity capital in the form of retained earnings does not entail flotation costs. However, it does involve an opportunity cost to the current shareholders. It is this economic cost that is calculated.

EXAMPLE: Find the cost of retained earnings for a firm that just paid a $1.50 annual dividend that is expected to grow 8% for the indefinite future, and whose current stock price is $30.

SOLUTION: Use equation 4.4:

$$k_s = \frac{\$1.50(1.08)}{\$30} + .08$$

$$= .054 + .08$$

$$= .134 \text{ or } \underline{13.4\%}$$

b. You could also use the *Capital Asset Pricing Model*, specifically, the *Security Market Line* (2.27):

$$k_s = R_F + \beta\left[E(R_M) - R_F\right] \qquad (4.5)$$

where:

R_F = the risk-free rate;

β = beta for the company;

$E(R_M)$ = expected market return.

EXAMPLE: Find the cost of retained earnings for a firm whose beta is 1.1, when the expected market return is 13% and the risk free rate is 6%.

SOLUTION: Use equation 4.5:

$$k_s = .06 + 1.1 * (.13 - .06)$$

$$= .06 + .077$$

$$= .137 \text{ or } \underline{13.7\%}$$

c. Finally, you can use the *bond plus risk premium* approach. This method involves finding the spread of the average stock over the bond issue, and then taking that spread and adding it to the particular firm's pre-tax cost of debt. The average stock has a beta of one, so its return is in essence the market return $E(R_M)$. You take the market return minus the yield on the average (typically single A rated) bond. This amount is then added to the company's cost of debt to get k_s.

2. The *cost of common equity*, in the form of *new issues of common stock*, k_e, differs from the cost for retained earnings because first, new stock issues must be sold at a discount from the current market price, and second, there are some flotation costs. These costs reduce the net proceeds to the firm, and therefore increase the cost of equity capital. It is usually estimated by using equation 4.4 above, and modifying for the additional costs:

$$k_e = \frac{D_1}{P_e - F} + g \qquad\qquad (4.6)$$

or

$$k_e = \frac{D_1}{P_e(1 - f)} + g \qquad\qquad (4.7)$$

where:
P_e = issue price of the new common stock;
F = other dollar flotation costs;
f = other flotation costs expressed as a fraction of the issue price.

Note that P_e is less than P_0 in equation 4.4.

3. The parameters D_1 and g can be estimated using techniques covered in Chapter 3. Please see pp. 39-41 for a discussion of these two.

III. ESTIMATING MARKET VALUE WEIGHTS
A. Assumptions
  1. A typical assumption in calculating market value weights is that the firm will raise new capital in the same proportions as are currently used by the company. This is to avoid potential feedback effects from changes in the capital structure to estimates for the cost of capital. For instance, increased use of debt may change the component costs of capital to reflect the change in risk.
  2. Instead of the previous assumption, one could assume that the firm has a target capital structure different from the current structure. In this case, however, one must further assume that the calculated component costs reflect that new structure.
  3. The formulas given above also assume that the various issues are simple; that is, there are no convertible features, attached warrants, etc., that might confuse the problem.
B. The weights should, when possible, be based on *market values*, not book values. Book values reflect the cost of balance sheet items at the time of purchase. Historical value may bear little relationship to current value in the market.
C. You must first find the market values of all components of long term capital:
  1. For actively traded debt, obtain a price quote from a bond dealer for each issue outstanding.
  2. If the bonds are not actively traded or have been privately placed, their market value will be difficult to estimate. You could check the prices of actively traded bond issues for similar companies. Keep in mind, however, that such quotes are only an estimate of true market value.
  3. For preferred equity and common equity, take the current market price per share and multiply it by the current number of shares outstanding. If the issue is not actively traded, then the quotes will be "stale" and may not represent current market value.

IV. ESTIMATING THE WEIGHTED AVERAGE COST OF CAPITAL (WACC)

A. The *weighted average cost of capital* (WACC) is given by the following equation:

$$WACC = \sum_i w_i k_i$$

$$WACC = w_d k_b (1 - T) + w_p k_p + w_e k_e \qquad (4.8)$$

where:
w_d = weight of debt;
k_b = pre-tax cost of debt;
w_p = weight of preferred stock;
k_p = cost of preferred stock;
w_e = weight of common equity;
k_c = cost of common equity.

EXAMPLE: A firm has a target capital structure of 30% debt, 10% preferred stock, and 60% equity. Its pre-tax cost of debt is 8%, preferred stock 10%, and retained earnings 14%. Its tax rate is 40%. Find its weighted average cost of capital.

SOLUTION: Using equation 4.8, we have:

$$WACC = .3*(1-.4)*8\% + .1*10\% + .6*14\%$$
$$= 1.44\% + 1\% + 8.4\%$$
$$= \underline{10.84\%}$$

V. LOCATING BREAK POINTS

A. A *break point* is the total amount of financing that a firm may raise using lower cost sources of funds before being forced to use a higher cost source. A break point occurs when a firm exhausts a low cost source of funds and must then substitute a higher cost source of the same type. A typical example is a firm's using up its available retained earnings to support expansion and being required to issue new shares of more expensive common stock.

B. Break points are found using the following formula:

$$Break\ Point = \frac{Amount\ Available\ from\ Source}{The\ Fraction\ of\ Capital\ the\ Source\ Represents} \quad (4.9)$$

Note that a break point includes the amount available from the source in question.

EXAMPLE: The company in the previous example has $20 million available in retained earnings. Common equity represents 60% of the company's capital structure. Find the break point associated with retained earnings.

SOLUTION: Using equation 4.9, we have:

$$\text{Break Point} = \frac{\$20\ million}{.6} = \underline{\$33.3\ million}$$

The firm can raise $13.3 million from preferred stock and bonds in addition to the $20 million from retained earnings. Beyond that point, it must issue new shares of common stock.

VI. THE MARGINAL COST OF CAPITAL SCHEDULE

A. As new higher cost sources of funding are substituted into the WACC, you follow the same procedure as before for finding the cost of capital above the break point as for below the break point.

B. The *marginal cost of capital* (MCC) is the cost of the next dollar of new capital that the firm raises. As the component costs rise, so does the MCC.

EXAMPLE: The firm in the previous two examples has a cost of capital of 10.84% below the break point of $33.3 million. A new external issue of common stock has a cost of 15%. Find the firm's cost of capital above the break point.

SOLUTION:

$$WACC_2 = .3*(1-.4)*8\%+.1*10\%+.6*15\%$$
$$= 1.44\%+1\%+9\%$$
$$= \underline{11.44\%}$$

VII. PROBLEMS WITH THE COST OF CAPITAL

A. A major problem with calculating the cost of capital is that it assumes that the new funds will be raised in exactly the same proportion as the firm currently uses. If this is not true, then the component costs may be different because the firm may have more (or less) risk from financial leverage. This problem is considered in Chapter 6.

B. A second problem is that the procedure above assumes that the additional assets that are being acquired with the new funds have a level of risk that is equal to the average risk of the assets on the balance sheet. If this is not true, then one must adjust the component costs to reflect the change in risk. This problem is addressed in Chapter 7.

CHAPTER 5
LEVERAGE

I. BASIC TERMS AND CONSIDERATIONS
  A. _Leverage_ is the use of fixed cost resources, either in the operations of a firm, or in its financing. The ultimate effect of leverage is to magnify profits or losses to the owners.
  B. _Business risk_ is the variability of a firm's operating income, or EBIT. It stems from several sources:
  1. Demand variability;
  2. Sales price variability;
  3. Input price variability;
  4. Flexibility in setting prices;
  5. Use of fixed cost methods of production.
  The variability in EBIT due to business risk also results in variability in the firm's earnings per share, or EPS.
  C. _Financial risk_ is the additional variability in the firm's earnings per share due to the use of debt in firm's capital structure.

II. OPERATING LEVERAGE
  A. _Operating leverage_ is the use of fixed cost methods of production.
  B. The _operating break-even point_ is that level of unit sales such that EBIT is equal to zero. If we assume linear revenue and variable cost functions, the break-even point is given by:

$$Q_{BE} = \frac{F}{P-V} \qquad\qquad (5.1)$$

  where:
  Q_{BE} = break-even unit sales;
  F = fixed costs;
  P = sales price per unit;
  V = variable cost per unit.

53

The breakeven point can also be expressed in terms of revenue by the following:

$$R_{BE} = Q_{BE} * P \tag{5.2}$$

where R_{BE} is the revenue breakeven point. This formula assumes that the product's sale price is fixed.

EXAMPLE: Find the break-even point for a firm whose fixed costs are $200,000, variable cost per unit is $8.00, and sales price per unit is $20.00.

SOLUTION: Using equation 5.1:

$$Q_{BE} = \frac{\$200,000}{\$20 - \$8}$$
$$= \underline{16,667 \text{ units}}$$

C. The *cash break-even point* is found by excluding non-cash fixed costs from total fixed costs:

$$Q_{CBE} = \frac{FC - Non\text{-}cash\ costs}{P - VC} \tag{5.3}$$

D. The Degree of Operating Leverage
   1. The *degree of operating leverage* (DOL) is the percentage change in EBIT for a given percentage change in unit sales:

$$DOL = \frac{\%\Delta EBIT}{\%\Delta SALES} = \frac{\dfrac{EBIT_2 - EBIT_1}{EBIT_1}}{\dfrac{SALES_2 - SALES_1}{SALES_1}} \tag{5.4}$$

   where:
   DOL = degree of operating leverage;
   EBIT = earnings before interest and taxes;
   %Δ = percentage change.

NOTE: The degree of operating leverage, indeed, all the degrees of leverage, including financial and combined, is an <u>elasticity</u>, as defined in economics. Thus any degree of leverage can be used to forecast the percentage change in one variable given a percentage change in the other.

EXAMPLE: At the current level of sales, a company's degree of operating leverage is 2.0, and EBIT is $700,000. If sales are forecast to rise 10%, what is the corresponding forecast for EBIT?

SOLUTION: A degree of operating leverage of 2.0 means that EBIT will rise 2% for each 1% change in sales volume. Thus a 10% change in sales volume means that EBIT will rise 20%. The forecasted EBIT is:

$$EBIT_2 = (1+.20)*\$700,000$$

$$= \underline{\$840,000}$$

2. A more useful computational formula for the degree of operating leverage is:

$$DOL = \frac{Q(P-V)}{Q(P-V)-F} \tag{5.5}$$

3. The above formula can also be expressed as:

$$DOL = \frac{Revenue - Total\ Variable\ Cost}{Revenue - Total\ Variable\ Cost - Fixed\ Cost} \tag{5.6}$$

EXAMPLE: Calculate the degree of operating leverage for a firm whose sales revenue is $1,000,000, variable costs are $400,000 at that level of sales, and fixed costs are $200,000.

SOLUTION: Using equation 5.6:

$$DOL = \frac{\$1,000,000 - \$400,000}{\$1,000,000 - \$400,000 - \$200,000}$$

$$= \underline{1.5}$$

NOTE: The degree of operating leverage is undefined at the break-even quantity Q_{BE} because the denominator is zero at that point.

III. FINANCIAL LEVERAGE
A. *Financial leverage* is the use of fixed cost methods of financing (that is, debt) in the capital structure of the firm.
B. Degree of Financial Leverage
1. *The degree of financial leverage* (DFL) is the percentage change in earnings per share (EPS) for a given percentage change in EBIT. Mathematically this is:

$$DFL = \frac{\%\Delta EPS}{\%\Delta EBIT} = \frac{\dfrac{EPS_2 - EPS_1}{EPS_1}}{\dfrac{EBIT_2 - EBIT_1}{EBIT_1}} \qquad (5.7)$$

2. A computational formula for DFL is:

$$DFL = \frac{EBIT}{EBIT - I} \qquad (5.8)$$

where:
I = interest expense.

EXAMPLE: Find the degree of financial leverage for a firm whose EBIT is $400,000 and interest expense is $250,000.

SOLUTION: Using equation 5.8:

$$DFL = \frac{\$400,000}{\$400,000 - \$250,000}$$

$$= \underline{2.67}$$

IV. COMBINED LEVERAGE

A. *Combined, or total, leverage* considers the overall effect of the use of any fixed cost resource on the earnings of the firm.

B. Degree of Combined Leverage

1. The *degree of combined leverage* (DCL) is the percentage change in earnings per share for a given percentage change in unit sales:

$$DCL = \frac{\% \Delta EPS}{\% \Delta SALES} = \frac{\dfrac{EPS_2 - EPS_1}{EPS_1}}{\dfrac{SALES_2 - SALES_1}{SALES_1}} \qquad (5.9)$$

2. An operational formula for the degree of combined leverage is:

$$DCL = \frac{Q(P-V)}{Q(P-V) - F - I} \qquad (5.10)$$

This can also be expressed as:

$$DCL = \frac{Sales \ - \ Total \ Variable \ Costs}{Sales \ - \ Total \ Variable \ Costs \ - \ Fixed \ Costs \ - \ Interest}$$

$$(5.11)$$

3. The degree of combined leverage is also the product of the degree of operating leverage and the degree of financial leverage:

$$DCL = DOL * DFL \qquad (5.12)$$

EXAMPLE: Find the degree of combined leverage for the firm examined in the previous two examples.
SOLUTION: Using equation 5.11:

$$DCL = \frac{\$1,000,000 - \$400,000}{\$1,000,000 - \$400,000 - \$200,000 - \$250,000}$$

$$= \underline{4.00}$$

You could also use equation 5.12:

$$DCL = 1.5 * 2.67$$

$$= \underline{4.00}$$

NOTE: The above formulas make it very clear that overall leverage is the result of operating <u>and</u> financial leverage. A high degree of combined leverage will have the same effect on earnings per share regardless of the individual degrees of operating and financial leverage. Therefore a firm's managers should not select its operating and financial leverage independently of each other, but rather with a particular degree of combined leverage in mind as a target.

V. INDIFFERENCE POINT ANALYSIS
   A. The *EPS indifference point* is the level of earnings before interest and taxes (EBIT) at which earnings per share would be equal under alternative methods of financing.

B. Mathematically, the EPS indifference point is defined as the EBIT that solves the following:

$$\frac{(EBIT - I_1)(1-T)}{S_1} = \frac{(EBIT - I_2)(1-T)}{S_2}$$

(5.13)

where:

I_i = interest under financing plan i;

S_i = number of shares of common stock outstanding under financing plan i.

Solving for EBIT, we get:

$$EBIT = \frac{I_1 - \dfrac{I_2}{S_2} * S_1}{1 - \dfrac{S_1}{S_2}}$$

(5.14)

EXAMPLE: A company is considering external financing. Plan 1 calls for 25 million new shares of common stock. Plan 2 calls for new debt that will increase interest payments from $20 million to $30 million, with the number of shares staying at 100 million. Its tax rate is 40%. Find the indifference EBIT.

SOLUTION: First identify the parameters:

PLAN 1	PLAN 2
$S_1 = 125$	$S_2 = 100$
$I_1 = 20$	$I_2 = 30$

Now use equation 5.14:

$$EBIT = \frac{20 - \dfrac{30}{100} * 125}{1 - \dfrac{125}{100}}$$

$$= \frac{17.5}{.25}$$

$$= \underline{\$70 \; million}$$

A check shows that the EPS is $0.24 under both plans at this level of EBIT.

C. The interpretation of the indifference point is that below this level of EBIT, the EPS would be higher under the plan to issue new common equity. Above this EBIT, the EPS would be higher under the plan to issue additional debt. Thus the indifference EBIT is a useful tool in financial planning. Given a forecast of EBIT, the planner can choose the financing plan that will maximize EPS.

CHAPTER 6
CAPITAL STRUCTURE
AND
FIRM VALUE

I. CAPITAL STRUCTURE
    A. The _capital structure_ of a firm is the permanent funding of the firm, consisting of long term debt, preferred stock, and common equity.

    B. _The optimal capital structure_ is that combination of debt and equity which maximizes the total value of the firm. The logical question then is, does there exist an optimal capital structure? Further, what does changing the capital structure do to the cost of capital?

II. EARLY APPROACHES TO CAPITAL STRUCTURE
    A. The _Net Operating Income_ approach assumes that the firm's overall cost of capital is constant. The market therefore values the entire firm rather than the components. As debt replaces equity in the capital structure, the cost of equity rises just enough to offset the cheaper debt.

    B. The _Traditional_ approach assumes that there is an optimal capital structure, and the firm can increase its value by moving toward that optimal structure.

      1. If the debt-equity ratio is below the optimal point, the substitution of debt for equity lowers the cost of capital, because the use of the cheaper debt more than offsets the higher cost of equity capital.

      2. If the debt-equity ratio is above the optimal value, then increased used of cheaper debt will not offset the rising cost of equity capital. Therefore firms should reduce their use of debt in such cases.

      3. This view is a version of what is called the _static tradeoff theory_, that is, capital structure decisions are determined by relative costs.

III. MODIGLIANI-MILLER WITHOUT TAXES

A. Modigliani and Miller (M&M) developed a model of capital structure that challenged the prevailing views in the late 1950s.

B. Assumptions of the Original Modigliani-Miller Model:

1. Markets for debt and equity are perfectly competitive, and securities are perfectly divisible.

2. There are no taxes of any sort.

3. Information is costlessly and instantaneously available.

4. Individuals can borrow at the same rate, k_d, as firms.

5. There are two firms U and L, which are identical in the following respects:

   a. total assets

   b. earnings

   c. risk

6. The two firms have a zero growth rate, and pay 100% of earnings as dividends.

7. The two firms differ only in their capital structure:

   a. Firm U is all equity financed, that is, it is unlevered.

   b. Firm L has debt as well as equity, i.e., it is levered.

C. Value of the Firm:

1. Under the above assumptions, M&M show that the value of a firm is independent of its capital structure:

$$V_U = V_L \tag{6.1}$$

where:

$$V_U = \frac{EBIT}{k_{sU}} \tag{6.2}$$

and:

V_U = value of the unlevered firm;

V_L = value of the levered firm;

k_{sU} = cost of equity for the unlevered firm.

2. The cost of equity k_{sL} for the levered firm L in a world without taxes is given by:

$$k_{sL} = k_{sU} + (k_{sU} - k_d)\left(D/S\right) \qquad (6.3)$$

where:

k_{sL} = cost of equity for the levered firm;
k_d = cost of debt;
D = market value of debt;
S = market value of equity.

3. There are three implications of this analysis:
   a. Capital structure has no effect on firm value.
   b. If there are no distortions (taxes, etc.) then the value of the firm is derived solely from its investments, that is, its assets.
   c. The cost of equity capital for the levered firm increases with the increased use of debt, but just enough to offset the use of the lower cost debt.

EXAMPLE: Find the values of firms U and L if EBIT is $1,000,000, k_{sU} is 10%, k_D is 6%, D = $4,000,000. Also find the cost of equity for the levered firm L.

SOLUTION: By equation 6.1, we know that the values of the two firms are equal. The value of the unlevered firm is given by equation 6.2:

$$V_U = \frac{\$1,000,000}{.1} = \underline{\$10,000,000}$$

Therefore the value of the levered firm L is also $10,000,000. By the balance sheet constraint, the value of the equity of the levered firm is $6,000,000. The cost of equity for the levered firm L is given by equation 6.3:

$$k_{sL} = .1 + (.1 - .06) * \frac{\$4,000,000}{\$6,000,000}$$

$$= .1 + .04 * (.6667)$$

$$= .12667 \text{ or } \underline{12.67\%}$$

As a check, we can find the value of the equity for the levered firm, using the cost of capital just found:

$$V_{sL} = \frac{\$1,000,000 - \$240,000}{.126667}$$

$$= \underline{\$6,000,000}$$

IV. MODIGLIANI-MILLER WITH TAXES

A. Modigliani and Miller revised their model to include corporate taxes and the tax-deductibility of interest. Keeping the rest of the assumptions, they then showed that the value of the firm is now a function of its capital structure:

$$V_L = V_U + TD \tag{6.4}$$

where:

$$V_U = \frac{EBIT(1 - T)}{k_{sU}} \tag{6.5}$$

and T is the corporate tax rate.

B. The cost of equity k_{SL} for a levered firm in a world with corporate taxes is given by:

$$k_{sL} = k_{sU} + (k_{sU} - k_d)(1 - T)\left(\frac{D}{S}\right) \tag{6.6}$$

C. The implications of including taxes in the analysis are:
   1. The "optimal" capital structure is as much debt as is possible.
   2. While the cost of equity capital rises with the increased leverage, the rise is slow enough so that the overall cost of capital falls with increased debt.
   3. The tax structure creates an imperfection that in turn can produce value.

EXAMPLE: Find the value of the firms given in the previous example, and the cost of equity for the levered firm, if the corporate tax rate is now 40%.

SOLUTION: The value of the unlevered firm is given by equation 6.5:

$$V_U = \frac{\$1,000,000*(1-.4)}{.1}$$
$$= \frac{\$600,000}{.1}$$
$$= \$6,000,000$$

The value of the levered firm is given by equation 6.4:

$$V_L = \$6,000,000 + .4*\$4,000,000$$
$$= \$7,600,000$$

The value of the levered firm's equity is therefore $3,600,000. We then find the cost of equity for the levered firm by using equation 6.6:

$$k_{sL} = .1 + (.1-.06)*(1-.4)*\frac{\$4,000,000}{\$3,600,000}$$
$$= .1 + (.04)*(.6)*1.1111$$
$$= .1267 \text{ or } 12.67\%$$

You can check the values by calculating the values of debt and equity directly using the costs of capital:

$$V_L = \frac{\$240,000}{.06} + \frac{(\$1,000,000 - \$240,000) * (1 - .4)}{.1267}$$

$$= \$4,000,000 + \$3,600,000$$

$$= \underline{\$7,600,000}$$

D. Capital Structure and the Capital Asset Pricing Model.
   1. Using the Capital Asset Pricing Model (CAPM), Hamada found the cost of equity k_{SL} for the levered firm to be given by the following:

$$k_{sL} = k_{RF} + (k_M - k_{RF}) * \beta_U + (k_M - k_{RF}) * \beta_U * (1 - T) * D/S$$

(6.7)

where:
k_{RF} = risk-free rate;
k_M = market rate;
β_U = beta for the firm with no leverage.

This result says that the cost of equity capital is the sum of the risk free rate, a premium for business risk, and a premium for financial risk.
   2. Hamada also derived the following expression for the beta of a levered firm:

$$\beta_L = \beta_U \left[1 + (1 - T) * D/S \right]$$

(6.8)

V. MILLER'S MODEL WITH PERSONAL TAXES
   A. Miller, without Modigliani, extended the analysis to a world in which there are both corporate and personal taxes. The value of a levered firm is given by:

$$V_L = V_U + \left[1 - \frac{(1 - T_c)(1 - T_s)}{(1 - T_D)}\right]D \tag{6.9}$$

where:

$$V_U = \frac{EBIT(1 - T_c)(1 - T_s)}{k_{sU}} \tag{6.10}$$

and:
T_C = corporate tax rate;
T_S = personal tax rate on stock income;
T_D = personal tax rate on debt income.

B. Some of the implications of this analysis are:
   1. If all tax rates are zero, the model reduces to the M&M propositions for a world of no taxes.
   2. If T_S and T_D are zero, the model reduces to the M&M propositions for a world with corporate taxes.
   3. In general, if T_S is less than T_D, the gain in firm value from leverage is less than it would be if they were equal.
   EXAMPLE: Find the values of the firms U and L considered in the two previous examples if T_S is 30% and T_D is 40%.
   SOLUTION: From equation 6.10, the value V_U of the unlevered firm is:

$$V_U = \frac{\$1,000,000 * (1 - .4) * (1 - .3)}{1 - .4}$$
$$= \$4,200,000$$

The value of the levered firm V_L is given by equation 6.9:

$$V_L = \$4,200,000 + \left[1 - \frac{(1-.4)*(1-.3)}{(1-.4)}\right] * \$4,000,000$$

$$= \$4,200,000 + (.3)*\$4,000,000$$

$$= \underline{\$5,400,000}$$

Note that the gain from leverage here is $1,200,000, as opposed to $3,600,000 in the world of corporate but no personal taxes.

VI. OTHER FACTORS AFFECTING CAPITAL STRUCTURE

A. The Modigliani and Miller models are termed static tradeoff models, because they balance the costs of capital and the value of tax shields against various other types of costs.

B. Financial Distress and Bankruptcy

1. The M&M analysis assumes away the costs of financial distress and bankruptcy. If it is possible for a firm to fail, then there may exist an optimal capital structure.

2. For debt-equity ratios above a certain level, the value of a tax shield resulting from the debt is more than offset by increasing expected costs of bankruptcy. The optimal capital structure is the point at which the value of expected bankruptcy costs equals the value of the tax shield

C. Agency Costs

1. An *agency cost* is one that arises when a security holder allows a manager to run a company in his or her place. The manager most likely has different desires than the security holder has, like a higher salary or nicer office.

2. In a capital structure model one security holder of interest is a bondholder. In order to protect his or her position as opposed to the position of the stockholders the bondholder will place restrictions on the actions of the

manager. Further, the bond holder must monitor the company to ensure the covenants are being followed.

   3. As the amount of debt increases, so does the monitoring cost. The net effect of these agency costs is to reduce the value of debt to the firm.

D. Signaling

   1. In a world of imperfect availability of information, a firm may attempt to *signal* the market by the type of security it issues.

   2. In general, a bond issue is taken as a positive signal by the market, because the existing owners would benefit from new profitable projects. A stock issue would signal the market that future prospects are not good, and the existing owners are seeking to spread their losses over new stock holders.

   3. Different results may occur, depending on the availability of information to various parties in the market.

E. The Pecking Order Hypothesis

   1. The *pecking order hypothesis* is a specific version of signaling.

   2. In general, it suggests that managers of firms have a preferred order in financing, based on the riskiness of the source to the managers of the firm:

      a. Retained earnings, which are the least risky because they do not entail bringing outsiders to monitor the firm;

      b. Debt, which is more risky to the firm than retained earnings but whose value fluctuates less than equity.

      c. New external capital, which is the riskiest of all to the firm because of the agency problems that arise.

F. In general, none of the theories presented offers a complete model of the capital structure decisions of a firm.

CHAPTER 7
CAPITAL BUDGETING

I. CAPITAL BUDGETING
    A. *Capital budgeting* is the process of identifying and evaluating real investment projects with a useful life greater than one year.

    B. The *objective of capital budgeting* is to select those projects which will maximize the value of the firm.

    C. The capital budgeting process involves five basic steps:
        1. Identify potential projects;
        2. Estimate the initial cost of the project;
        3. Estimate the expected benefits from the project;
        4. Evaluate the acceptability of the project;
        5. Review the project periodically.

II. CASH FLOW ESTIMATION
    A. In evaluating a capital budgeting project, the relevant benefits are those that are *after-tax, incremental, cash flows*. The relevant costs are *after-tax incremental cash expenses*.
        1. Costs and benefits should be measured on an <u>after-tax basis</u> to reflect what the firm really pays and collects.
        2. Costs and benefits should be measured <u>incrementally</u>, that is, the additional costs and benefits that are attributable to the proposed project.
        3. Benefits should include those resulting from the <u>operation</u> of the project, but not from its financing.
        4. Costs and benefits should be measured by <u>cash flows</u>, because ultimately all receipts and payments must be in cash.

    B. These basic considerations lead to the following rules:
        1. You should not consider any *sunk costs* in capital budgeting. These costs have no impact on future cash flows from the project, and are not attributable to the project as defined at time zero.

2. You should not include *interest expense* in the cash flows from a project. Interest expense is a financing cash flow, not an operating cash flow. The interest cost that might be incurred in financing the project is considered in the weighted average cost of capital.

3. You should include the *opportunity costs* of the resources used.

4. You should also include the *external effects* of the project on the cash flows from the rest of the firm's operations.

C. The *net investment* (NINV) is the initial net cash outflow associated with the project. It consists of the depreciable basis (DB), the net salvage value (NSV) of any old assets that are sold, and any changes in net working capital (ΔWC):

$$NINV = DB + NSV + \Delta WC \qquad (7.1)$$

1. The *depreciable basis* is equal to the purchase price of the asset, plus shipping and installation. In effect, it is any cost that is necessary to put the asset into use. The depreciable basis is not adjusted for the estimated salvage value at the end of the project's useful life.

2. *Net salvage value* is the proceeds from the sale of an existing asset, adjusted for any tax effects. Tax effects will arise if the market value (MV) is different from the book value (BV) or depreciated value of the asset. There are four possible cases:

a. If book value equals market value (BV=MV), then there is no tax effect, and the net salvage value equals the sale proceeds.

b. If book value is greater than market value (BV>MV), the old asset is sold at a loss. The difference MV-BV is treated as an operating loss and thus reduces taxable income. This reduces taxes and increases cash flow. The net salvage value from the sale of the old asset is:

$$NSV = MV + T*(BV - MV) \qquad (7.2)$$

where T is the firm's tax rate on ordinary income.

c. If book value is less than market value (BV<MV), the old asset is sold at a gain. The difference MV-BV is treated as operating income and taxed as such. The net salvage value is:

$$NSV = BV + (1-T)*(MV - BV) \qquad (7.3)$$

d. If the market value exceeds the original cost (OC) of the asset (MV>OC>BV), the amount original cost minus book value is treated as operating income, and the excess of market value over original cost is treated as a capital gain. The net salvage value is:

$$NSV = BV + (1-G)*(MV - OC) + (1-T)*(OC - BV)$$

$$(7.4)$$

where G is the firm's tax rate on capital gains.

3. The *net addition to working capital* is the amount the firm must increase its current assets over current liabilities at the start of the project. This increase could be the result of increased inventories to meet new sales or increased cash balances at new retail outlets, among other reasons. These activities all require cash and therefore should be included in the net investment. It is defined as:

$$\Delta WC = \Delta CA - \Delta CL \qquad (7.5)$$

where:
CA = current assets;
CL = current liabilities.

D. The *expected benefits of the project* are the net incremental after-tax operating cash flows the project will generate, plus any non-operating cash flows directly resulting from the project. These non-operating cash flows include those resulting from the salvage value of the new asset at the end of its useful life, as well as the recovery of the net investment of working capital that may occur at the end of the project. As noted above, the benefits should not include interest expense.

1. In general, the yearly operating cash flows are defined as the following incremental cash flows:

$$\Delta CF_t = \Delta NI_t + \Delta Dep_t \qquad (7.6)$$

where:
ΔCF = change in cash flows resulting from the project;
ΔNI = change in net income due to the project;
ΔDep = change in depreciation due to the project;
  t = time.

2. The following template is useful in determining the net operating benefits in a given year:

ΔRevenues
- *ΔCash Operating Expenses*
= *ΔEarnings before Depreciation, Interest and Taxes*
- *ΔDepreciation*
= *ΔEarnings before Interest and Taxes*
- *ΔTaxes*
- *ΔNI*
+ *ΔDepreciation*
= *ΔBenefits*

3. The most important part of capital budgeting is forecasting operating earnings, or earnings before depreciation, interest, and taxes (EBDIT). This will

depreciation, interest, and taxes (EBDIT). This will typically require a forecast of sales for several years to come, which is always a difficult process. Operating expenses may also be a function of sales, so an extensive analysis of costs will probably also be required.

4. *Depreciation* is the procedure in which the cost of a capital asset is allocated over its life. It is a non-cash expense that reduces the taxable income of the firm, and thus increases its cash flow.

   a. Depreciation charges are based on the asset's depreciable basis (see p.72.)

   b. Under current tax law, the depreciation charges in any period may be based on the *modified accelerated cost recovery system* (MACRS). Assets are allocated to a particular class, and depreciation charges are calculated using the percentages for that class.

   c. MACRS also uses the half-year convention. Under this, the asset is assumed to go into use on July 1 of the first year. Therefore the firm is allowed one-half of the year's depreciation. This means there is always one more year's worth of depreciation charges than the class of the asset. For example, an asset in the 5 year class will generate depreciation charges in 6 calendar years. Table A.5. shows the depreciation rates for various classes of assets.

5. Non-operating cash flows include:

   a. The after-tax salvage value in the terminal year of the asset under consideration

   b. Recovery of the net investment in working capital made at the beginning of the project or throughout its life.

III. METHODS OF EVALUATION

A. Payback

   1. The *payback* of a project is the time it takes the project to generate cash flows sufficient to recover the net investment on a non-discounted basis.

is whatever the decision maker says it is.
3. The advantages of the payback method are:
a. It easy to calculate.
b. It is easy to understand.
4. The disadvantages of payback are:
a. It does not have an objective criterion for selecting projects.
b. It does not necessarily maximize the value of the firm.
c. It does not consider time value of money.
d. It ignores cash flows beyond payback period.
B. Accounting Rate of Return
1. The *accounting rate of return* (ARR) measures a project's return to investment. It is defined as:

$$ARR = \frac{Average\ annual\ income}{Average\ investment} \qquad (7.7)$$

2. The advantage of ARR is that it is simple to calculate.
3. The disadvantages are:
a. It does not have an objective decision rule.
b. It is based on income, not cash flow.
c. It does not take time value into account.
C. Net Present Value (NPV)
1. The *net present value* (NPV) of a project is defined as:

$$NPV = \sum_{t=1}^{N} \frac{\Delta CF_t}{(1+k)^t} - NINV \qquad (7.8)$$

where:
ΔCF_t = incremental cash flow from the project at time t;
k = firm's cost of capital;
NINV = initial net investment at time zero.

2. The decision rules for NPV are:
a. If NPV > 0, accept the project.
b. If NPV < 0, reject the project.

b. If NPV < 0, reject the project.
3. The advantages of NPV are:
   a. It has an objective decision rule.
   b. Applied correctly, it will lead to the selection of projects that maximize the value of the firm.
   c. It considers all operating cash flows.
   d. It considers the time value of money.
4. The disadvantages of NPV are:
   a. Some inputs are difficult to calculate or construct.
   b. Risk may not be correctly accounted for.
D. Internal Rate of Return
   1. The *internal rate of return* (IRR) for a project is the discount rate that sets the net present value of a project equal to zero:

$$\sum_{t=1}^{N} \frac{\Delta CF_t}{(1+IRR)^t} - NINV = 0 \qquad (7.9)$$

   2. The decision rules for IRR are:
      a. If the IRR > k, where k is the firm's cost of capital, accept the project.
      b. If the IRR < k, reject the project.
   3. The advantages of IRR are:
      a. It has an objective decision rule.
      b. It considers all relevant cash flows.
      c. It considers the time value of money.
   4. The disadvantages of IRR are:
      a. It does not always select projects that maximize the value of the firm.
      b. It is difficult to solve for IRR without a calculator.
      c. There may be more than one IRR for a project, which makes the decision process more complicated.
E. Modified Internal Rate of Return
   1. The *modified internal rate of return* (MIRR) is the discount rate that sets the terminal value of the cash flows of the project equal to the initial investment. This

terminal value TV_N of the project's cash flows is found by assuming reinvestment at the firm's cost of capital:

$$TV_N = \sum_{t=1}^{N} \Delta CF_t * (1+k)^{N-t} \qquad (7.10)$$

Then use TV_N to solve for MIRR:

$$TV_N = NINV * (1 + MIRR)^N$$

Solving for MIRR, we get:

$$MIRR = \left(\frac{TV_N}{NINV}\right)^{\frac{1}{N}} - 1 \qquad (7.11)$$

2.. The decision rules for MIRR are similar to IRR's:
    a. If MIRR > k, accept the project;
    b. If MIRR < k, reject the project.
3. The advantages of MIRR are:
    a. It has a more reasonable reinvestment rate assumption than IRR.
    b. It generally gives a single solution.
4. Its major disadvantage is it may not select value maximizing projects.
F. Profitability Index
    1. The *profitability index* (PI) is the ratio of the present value of the benefits to the net investment:

$$PI = \frac{\displaystyle\sum_{t=1}^{N} \frac{\Delta CF_t}{(1+k)^t}}{NINV} \qquad (7.12)$$

2. The decision rules for the profitability index are:
    a. If PI > 1, accept the project.
    b. If PI < 1, reject the project.

3. The advantages of the PI are:
   a. It considers time value of money;
   b. It has an objective decision rule;
   c. It can be useful in situations of capital rationing.
4. Its major disadvantages are:
   a. It may not necessarily select value maximizing projects.
   b. It may conflict with other discounted cash flow methods in selecting projects.

G. If the cash flows from a project are "normal", that is, a single cash outflow at time zero, followed by a series of positive cash flows, then all the *discounted cash flow* (DCF) methods (NPV, IRR, MIRR, and PI) give the same accept/reject decision for independent projects. If one method indicates that the project should be accepted, then all methods will indicate acceptance. You should note, however, that there are cases involving unusual patterns of cash flows in which the rules can give conflicting decisions.

EXAMPLE: Suppose a project has a net investment (NINV) and depreciable basis of $100,000. It is in the 3 year MACRS class but will generate additional earnings before depreciation and tax of $50,000 for the next 4 years. The firm is in the 40% tax bracket and its cost of capital is 10%. Calculate the cash flows for each of the next four years, then evaluate the acceptability of the project using each of the methods given above.

SOLUTION: The cash flows are:

YEAR	1	2	3	4
ΔEBDT	50,000	50,000	50,000	50,000
- ΔDEP	33,000	45,000	15,000	7,000
=ΔEBT	17,000	5,000	35,000	43,000
- ΔTAX	6,800	2,000	14,000	17,200
=ΔEAT	10,200	3,000	21,000	25,800
+ΔDEP	33,000	45,000	15,000	7,000
=ΔCF	43,200	48,000	36,000	32,800

(Note: the depreciation charges are based on rounded percentages given in Table A.5, rather than out to two decimal places for simplicity.)

The payback is 2.24 years.

The accounting rate of return is calculated as

$$ARR = \frac{\dfrac{(10{,}200 + 3{,}000 + 21{,}000 + 25{,}800)}{4}}{\dfrac{(100{,}000 - 0)}{2}}$$

$$= \frac{15{,}000}{50{,}000} = \underline{30\%}$$

Net present value is:

$$NPV = \frac{43{,}200}{1.10} + \frac{48{,}000}{(1.10)^2} + \frac{36{,}000}{(1.10)^3} + \frac{32{,}800}{(1.10)^4} - 100{,}000$$
$$= 128{,}392 - 100{,}000$$
$$= \underline{+28{,}392}$$

The IRR is the solution to the following:

$$0 = \frac{43{,}200}{1 + IRR} + \frac{48{,}000}{(1 + IRR)^2} + \frac{36{,}000}{(1 + IRR)^3} + \frac{32{,}800}{(1 + IRR)^4} - 100{,}000$$

At 20% the NPV is +5,984 and at 25%, it is -2,853. Using equation 1.20 for linear interpolation we have:

$$IRR = \frac{5,984-0}{5,984-(-2,853)}*(25-20)+20$$

$$=.6772*5+20$$

$$=\underline{23.38\%}$$

A hand calculator gives 23.30%.

The MIRR is found by first calculating the terminal value of the cash flows, using the cost of capital:

$$TV_4 = 43,200*(1.10)^3 + 48,000*(1.10)^2$$

$$+36,000*(1.10)^1 + 32,800*(1.10)^0$$

$$= 57,499+58,080+39,600+32,800$$

$$= \underline{187,979}$$

Using equation 7.11, we then solve for MIRR:

$$187,979 = 100,000*(1+MIRR)^4$$

$$MIRR = (1.87979)^{\frac{1}{4}} - 1$$

$$= \underline{17.09\%}$$

The PI is found as:

$$PI = \frac{128,392}{100,000}$$

$$= \underline{1.284}$$

All the discounted cash flow methods (NPV, IRR, MIRR, and PI) indicate the project should be accepted. No decision can be made on the basis of the payback or the ARR because not enough information was given.

IV. SPECIAL PROBLEMS IN CAPITAL BUDGETING
A. Conflicts Between Decision Rules
  1. Conflicts between accounting based measures (e.g., payback or accounting rate of return) and discounted cash flow methods (IRR, NPV, etc.) in ranking projects are common and should always be resolved in favor of the DCF recommendation.
  2. Conflicts between various DCF measures in ranking projects also occur frequently. The methods usually give the same accept/reject decision for individual independent projects (see above). Problems occur in ranking mutually exclusive projects from most desirable to least desirable. There are several reasons why conflicts will arise:
    a. Unequal scale of projects. Small projects tend to have high IRRs but low NPVs.
    b. Multiple IRRs. If a project has "unusual" cash flows, e.g., negative cash flows in some years, it can have several IRRs. The question then becomes, which IRR do you use?
    c. Reinvestment rate. The IRR uses the IRR itself as the reinvestment rate for all cash flows. This in effect is the same as assuming that the firm has a series of projects that the firm can reinvest in, all with the same IRR.
  3. The general solution to such problems is to use NPV. Using NPV solves all the problems just stated:
    a. The higher the NPV, the greater the addition to the firm's net worth.
    b. There is only one NPV, not multiple ones.
    c. The NPV assumes reinvestment at the firm's cost of capital, which is a much more reasonable assumption.
B. A *replacement decision* involves the substitution of a newer asset for an older asset. The analysis follows the same basic rules given above. The only significant differences are that the cash inflows are typically reductions in cash operating cash flows and changes in depreciation, and there may be salvage value from the old machine.

C. Projects with Unequal Lives
  1. If projects have useful lives that are different, net present value must be calculated in a way that eliminates the effect of the difference.
  2. There are two methods you can use:
    a. The *replacement chain* approach requires finding the least common multiple of the useful lives, and then assuming that each project can be replicated over that number of years. Projects are then compared on the basis of the NPVs for the (assumed) common lifetime.
    b. The *equivalent annual annuity* approach requires the following steps:
      1. Find the NPV of each project.
      2. Calculate the annuity over the life of each project that has the same NPV.
      3. Assume the annuities found in 2 are perpetuities and value them using equation 1.14 for the present value of a perpetuity.
D. Inflation
  1. Inflation can introduce a bias into capital budgeting if cash flows and discount rates are not treated consistently.
  2. Again there are two ways to adjust for inflation:
    a. Calculate all cash flows in real terms, that is, with the price increases removed. Then use a real cost of capital, one with the expected inflation premium removed.
    b. Calculate all cash flows with an explicit inflation forecast, and then use the nominal cost of capital.

V. RISK IN CAPITAL BUDGETING
  A. The riskiness of a project depends on its relationship to rest of the firm's assets.
    1. *Stand-alone risk* refers to the situation in which the riskiness of the project is evaluated in isolation from the rest of the firm. This is proper only if the project is the single asset of the firm. In this case, the proper measure of risk is the variance of the project's possible returns, as

given by equation 2.12 or 2.13, p.20, or the standard
deviation.
2. *Within-firm risk* refers to the situation in which the
project will be included in a portfolio of assets. In this
case, the proper measure of risk is the variance of a
portfolio, equation 2.22, p.23, or the standard deviation,
equation 2.24, p.23.
3. *Market risk* refers to the situation in which the project
will be included in a well-diversified portfolio of assets
that approximates the market portfolio. In this case, the
proper measure of risk is the project's beta, as defined
in equation 2.28, p.26.
B. Adjusting for Risk
1. The *certainty equivalent method* (CEM) adjusts the cash
flows of a project to reflect project's risk each year.
2. The *risk adjusted discount rate approach* (RADR)
modifies the discount rate to reflect the difference in the
level of risk of the project from that of the average
riskiness of the firm. The higher the project's risk, the
higher the discount rate. There are several ways this can
be accomplished:
a. Subjectively, by using some relative risk measure to
create different risk categories. For instance, you could
use the coefficient of variation to allocate projects to
one of several risk groups, each one with a subjectively
determined discount rate.
b. More rigorously, by explicitly accounting for the risk by
using the project's beta to calculate its required return.

CHAPTER 8
DIVIDEND POLICY

I. BASIC CONSIDERATIONS

    A. A *dividend* is a distribution made by a firm to its stockholders. It is typically a cash distribution, but may also be additional shares of stock.

    B. *Dividend policy* refers to the decisions a company makes concerning the type, size, and timing of the distributions made to the common stockholders.

    C. The *optimal dividend policy* is that policy which maximizes the market value of the firm.

II. PAYMENT PROCEDURE

    A. The *declaration date* is the day on which the Board of Directors votes to pay a dividend.

    B. The *ex-dividend date* is the first day on which the stock trades without the right to the most recently declared dividend.

    C. The *holder-of-record date* is the day on which the ownership of the stock is determined. It is four business days after the ex-dividend day.

    D. The *payment date* is the day on which the dividend is actually paid.

III. FACTORS AFFECTING DIVIDEND POLICY

    A. Ultimately, dividends are paid from *earnings*. The long term earnings behavior will be the major determinant of a firm's ability to pay a dividend. Short term or temporary fluctuations in earnings will exert little influence on a firm's dividend decision, so long as such fluctuations don't affect the firm's cash or impair capital (see below).

    B. A firm's *available cash* will limit its ability to pay a cash dividend. A firm may have excellent earnings but be short of cash, and therefore be unable to pay a cash dividend.

    C. The greater a firm's *growth opportunities*, the smaller its dividend. A firm will thus choose to retain a greater percentage of its earnings to fund the growth.

D. Some institutional investors are restricted to holding stocks that pay a dividend and therefore appear on *legal lists*. Given the increasing importance of institutional investors in the market, firms may well choose to pay at least a small dividend in order to appear on these lists.

E. Firms are generally restricted from paying a dividend that would reduce its paid-in capital. These *capital impairment* rules are to protect creditors from a firm's essentially paying out a liquidating dividend ahead of interest and principal to the creditors.

F. *Loan restrictions or bond covenants* may prohibit firms from paying a dividend in excess of a certain amount.

G. Companies with certain characteristics appeal to different groups of investors or *clienteles*. For instance, utilities pay a large dividend and attract investors looking for safe income. A change in that policy may lead existing investors to sell the stock.

H. *Taxes* may also influence a firm's decision to pay a dividend. Dividend income and capital gains may be taxed at different rates. Furthermore, IRS rules against improper accumulation of earnings may also lead firms to pay a dividend.

I. A firm's *access to capital markets* may affect dividend policy. Smaller firms with limited access may choose not to pay a dividend and instead retain all earnings as the major source of equity capital.

IV. THEORIES CONCERNING DIVIDENDS AND THE VALUE OF THE FIRM

A. One line of argument is that dividends should be irrelevant in determining the value of a firm. Miller and Modigliani, in a companion piece to their articles on capital structure, demonstrated the *irrelevance of dividend policy* under the assumptions of perfect markets and no taxes. That is, neither the level nor the timing of the dividend has any impact on the value of firm.

B. Arguments for the Relevance of Dividends

    1. The *dividend discount model* (DDM) as presented in Chapter 3 suggests that the greater the dividends a firm pays, all else held equal, the greater the value of the firm.

    2. *Clientele effects* may influence dividend decisions. That is, some investors may prefer to invest in firms with higher growth potential and therefore pay lower dividends. Others may prefer current income, and thus invest in companies with high payout ratios.

    3. *Differences in tax rates* for stockholders between dividend income and capital gains income may influence firms to retain more earnings and thus pay a smaller dividend. This is especially true for firms with a few large stockholders who are taxed.

    4. Dividends may *reduce the uncertainty* about cash flows and therefore may be preferred by investors.

    5. Dividends may also contain *information* about the future of the firm, and the firm uses dividend policy to signal the market about such information. In general, these theories suggest that it is the *unanticipated change* in the dividend that counts. For instance, an increased dividend would normally be a signal that the firm feels confident about its future and is signaling this confidence through the increase in the dividend.

V. DIVIDEND POLICY IN PRACTICE

A. The *residual dividend policy* states that a firm should only pay a dividend after it has funded all profitable investment projects. The size of a dividend depends upon the firm's investment opportunity schedule as well as its earnings.

B. A *stable dollar dividend policy* is one in which the firm pays the same amount per share for a period of time, raising it only after earnings have risen enough to justify a change.

C. A <u>*stable payout ratio policy*</u> is one in which the firm pays out the same percentage of net income. The dollar amount therefore varies from period to period with net income.

D. A <u>*low regular plus large extra dividend policy*</u> is one in which the firm pays a low, stable dollar amount per share every period and a larger bonus dividend as earnings permit.

VI. RELATED ISSUES

A. A <u>*stock split*</u> is a change in the number of shares outstanding that is accomplished by a change in par value. For example, a 2-for-1 split cuts the par value in half and creates twice the number of shares than before the split.

B. A <u>*stock dividend*</u> is the payment of additional shares of stock in the place of, or in addition to, the regular cash dividend. A stock dividend is accounted for by increasing the number of shares outstanding, increasing the common stock value at par and reducing the retained earnings account. In essence, it is a transfer from retained earnings to common stock on the balance sheet.

NOTE: While the accounting treatments are different, neither a stock split nor a stock dividend in and of itself changes shareholder wealth. The percentage change in the number of shares is exactly offset by the percentage change in the market price.

CHAPTER 9
LONG TERM FINANCING

I. BONDS

A. A _bond_ is form of long term debt issued by any of a variety of borrowers like the Federal Government and corporations.

B. Terms of a bond are stated in the _indenture_, or legal contract. A bond indenture will typically include:

  1. The bond's _par value_, or the amount that will be repaid at maturity. Most corporate and Treasury bonds have a par value of $1,000, while many municipal bonds have a par value of $5,000.

  2. The _coupon rate_, the percentage of par value that the borrower will pay in interest annually.

  3. The _maturity date_ is the date on which the principal amount is due. Most bonds have maturities between ten and thirty years, although there are bonds that have forty-year maturities or longer.

In addition, the indenture will also specify the following:

  4. The trustee, usually a financial institution that will represent bondholders in any legal proceedings.

  5. The paying agent, an institution that will be responsible for disbursing the interest and principal payments.

  6. The permissible methods of retirement of the bond, which may take several forms:

    a. Repayment of principal at maturity.

    b. Through a _sinking fund_, in which the issuer retires a certain amount of the issue every year, with the specific bonds retired being selected at random.

    c. Through a _serial bond_ issue.

    d. Through a _call_, in which the issuer redeems the entire issue before maturity at a price above par. This "call price is set in the indenture.

    e. Through _conversion_ of the bond into shares of common stock at the option of the bondholder.

    f. Through the exercise of a _warrant_, in which the

f. Through the exercise of a _warrant_, in which the bondholder trades in the bond and buys shares of common stock.

7. The type of collateral, if any.

D. Types of Bonds

1. A _debenture_ is a bond that is unsecured by any collateral.

   a. A _senior debenture_ is one that has priority in repayment in bankruptcy before other unsecured bonds.

   b. A _subordinated debenture_ is one that is paid off after senior bonds in the event of a bankruptcy.

2. A _mortgage bond_ is one secured by real property.

3. An _income bond_ is one in which interest is paid only if firm makes a specific level of earnings.

4. A _zero-coupon bond_ is one that pays no interest during its term, only its principal at maturity.

5. A _floating rate bond_ is one whose coupon is periodically adjusted to reflect current market rates

E. Advantages and Disadvantages of Bond Financing

1. The advantages of bond financing include:

   a. The payment per period is fixed.

   b. It increases leverage, which will magnify earnings for the company's owners.

   c. It is typically the cheapest form of financing

   d. Interest is deductible for federal income tax purposes.

   e. Up to a point, use of debt financing may lower the firm's cost of capital.

2. The disadvantages include:

   a. The fixed payment must be made, or bankruptcy could result.

   b. The increased leverage would magnify any losses for the company's owners.

   c. The increased leverage could increase risk, and therefore increase the cost of other sources of capital.

   d. Beyond a certain level, increased used of debt can cause the firm's cost of capital to rise.

1. Many bonds are evaluated by one or more of several ratings agencies, including Moody's, Standard and Poor's, and Fitch's. These ratings convey information to the market about the potential default risk of the bond.
2. The bond ratings of the agencies are similar. Those for Moody's and Standard and Poor's are:

Moody's	**S&P**	
Aaa	AAA	Highest Quality
Aa	AA	High Quality
A	A	Upper Medium Grade
Baa	BBB	Medium Grade
Ba	BB	Lower Medium Grade
B	B	Speculative
Caa	CCC	More Speculative
Ca	CC	and
C		High Risk of Default
	C	Income bond
	D	In Default

3. Bonds with a rating of Baa/BBB or higher are called *investment grade bonds*. Those with ratings of Ba/BB or lower are called *speculative grade*, or *high yield*, or *"junk" bonds*.

II. PREFERRED STOCK

A. *Preferred stock* is a form of equity that has priority of claim over common stock with respect to earnings and, in the dissolution of the firm, to distribution of assets.
B. Preferred stock typically has the following features:
   1. It is non-voting, that is, owners of preferred shares do not have a say in the election of the Board of Directors or in matters of corporate governance.
   2. It has a fixed payment, or dividend.
   3. The dividend may be omitted without the firm's being forced into bankruptcy. Omission of a preferred dividend

forced into bankruptcy. Omission of a preferred dividend prevents the firm from paying a common stock dividend. If the preferred dividend is omitted, it may be *cumulative*, that is, omitted dividends must be repaid in full before common stock dividends may be resumed.

4. It has no maturity date.

5. It is *non-participating*, that is, it does not share in any increased earnings of the firm

C. Preferred stock is sometimes called a *hybrid security*, because it has features of both debt and equity.

1. Technically it is a form of equity, so from a legal point of view it is included in the equity accounts.

2. It has a fixed payment, which is similar to the coupon paid on bonds. This fixed payment increases the firm's financial leverage.

D. Advantages and Disadvantages of Preferred Stock

1. The advantages of preferred stock financing include:

a. It usually has a fixed dividend.

b. It can increase the leverage of earnings to common stockholders.

c. Failure to make the payment does not result in bankruptcy.

2. Disadvantages of preferred stock financing include:

a. It carries a higher pre-tax cost than debt.

b. The dividend is not tax deductible.

c. The dividend must be paid before any common stock dividends can be paid.

III. COMMON STOCK

A. *Common stock* represents the residual ownership of a company. Common stock typically has the following features:

1. It is permanent, that is, it has no maturity date.

2. It has a proportional residual claim against income.

3. It has final claim against assets in the event of liquidation.

4. It has *limited liability*, that is, a common stock investor

can lose no more than 100% of his or her investment.

5. It has the *preemptive right* in the event of a new issue of additional common stock. That means that a current stockholder has the right to purchase new shares before the general public sufficient to maintain his or her proportional ownership. See the section on rights offerings below.

6. It generally has the right to vote for the board of directors and on other corporate business. This may not be true if the company has dual class stock, in which one class carries the right to the residual income and the other carries the voting rights.

B. Advantages and Disadvantages of Common Stock

1. The advantages of common stock financing include:
   a. It is permanent.
   b. It entails no fixed or required payment.
   c. It may reduce the riskiness of the firm, and thus reduce the cost of future financing.

2. Disadvantages of common stock financing include:
   a. It dilutes the ownership and earning per share of the firm.
   b. It reduces the leverage of the firm.
   c. It is the highest cost source of funding.

C. An *Initial Public Offering* (IPO) is the first issue of the company's common stock to be sold to the public. It also referred to as taking the commpany public or going public.

D. Rights Offerings

1. A *rights offering* is the sale of additional shares of common stock by giving the current shareholders the right to buy new shares before the general public.

2. The procedure is typically as follows:

3. The value of a right can be found from the following:
   a. If the stock is trading *rights on*, that is, with the ownership of the rights still attached to the common stock, then the value of a right is:

$$v_{on} = \frac{P_0 - P_s}{N+1}$$ (9.1)

where:
    P_0 = current market price of the stock, rights on;
    P_s = subscription price;
    N = number of shares needed to buy one new share.

  b. If the stock is trading *ex-rights*, then the value of a right is given by:

$$v_{ex} = \frac{P_0 - P_s}{N}$$ (9.2)

IV. RELATED INSTRUMENTS AND PRACTICES
A. Convertible Securities
  1. A *convertible security* is an instrument, either preferred stock or a bond, that can be exchanged for the company's common stock at the option of the security holder.
  2. The *conversion ratio* (CR) is the number of shares of common stock that will be received per bond.
  3. The *conversion price* (CP) is the effective price the investor pays for the shares upon conversion. The relationship between conversion ratio and conversion price is:

$$CR = \frac{Par\ Value}{CP}$$ (9.3)

  4. The *investment*, or *straight bond*, value of a convertible is the price the bond would sell for without the conversion feature. This is found by discounting the bond's interest and principal payments at the market yield of similar debt.
  5. The *conversion value* (CV) is the value of the number of shares that would be received at conversion at current market prices:

$$CV = CR * P_M \qquad\qquad (9.4)$$

where P_M is the current market price of the stock.

6. The *conversion premium* is the excess of the market value over conversion value, in percentage terms:

$$\text{Premium} = \frac{P_M - CV}{CV} \qquad\qquad (9.5)$$

7. A convertible security has the following advantages:
   a. It typically has a lower coupon (or dividend, for preferred stock) than a non-convertible security because of the conversion option.
   b. The conversion feature allows the firm to reduce its leverage if it performs well and investors choose to convert.
8. A convertible security has the following disadvantages:
   a. The convertible feature poses a potential dilution of ownership.
   b. If the firm does not do well, then it will be saddled with the debt because investors will not convert.

B. Warrants
   1. A *warrant* is option that gives the holder the right to purchase shares of stock of the issuing company. A warrant is different from an exchange traded option and from convertible securities in several respects:
      a. It is usually longer term.
      b. It is written by the issuing company.
      c. Exercise of the warrant requires an additional payment of cash from the investor to the firm.
   2. The *value of a warrant* is equal to its intrinsic value plus its time value.
      a. The *intrinsic* or *minimum value* V_W is:

$$V_W = \frac{(P_0 - EP)}{N} \tag{9.6}$$

where:
P_0 = current price of the stock;
EP = exercise price of the warrant;
N = number of warrants needed to purchase one share of common stock.

  b. The *time value* is the difference between the market value and the intrinsic value of the warrant. In general, it is a function of the time to expiration, volatility, and the leverage inherent in the warrant.
C. Bond Refunding
  1. A *bond refunding* is the process of calling an existing issue and replacing it with a new issue with a lower coupon.
  2. A refunding decision can be evaluated as a capital budgeting decision.
    a. The *cost of refunding* (net investment) includes the call premium, the tax savings from the unexpensed flotation costs of the old issue, and the net interest that is paid while both issues are outstanding.
    b. The *benefits* are the reduced after-tax interest payments, and the amortized flotation expenses from the new issue.
    c. The *appropriate discount rate* is the after-tax cost of the new debt.

V. NON-MARKET SOURCES OF LONG TERM FUNDS
A. Term Loan
  1. A *term loan* is a bank loan with an initial maturity greater than one year.
  2. A term loan typically has the following characteristics:
    a. The interest rate is typically a floating rate, and is usually computed as a spread over the prime rate.

b. It is *amortized*, that is, principal is paid back in installments over the life of the loan. In some cases, there may be a balloon payment left at the end of the loan term.

c. It is usually *secured* by some collateral.

d. By definition, the *maturity* is greater than one year. In practice, the maturity is typically between five and ten years.

e. There are extensive covenants and restrictions.

B. Leasing

1. *Leasing* is the renting of assets as opposed to owning them outright. There are several types of leases, of which the most important are:

    a. Operating lease,

    b. Financial, or capital, lease,

2. According to FASB 13, under certain circumstances, a lease must be capitalized, that is, the value of the item leased must be shown as an asset and the lease itself shown as a liability on the lessee's books. The lease is classified as a capital lease if any one of the following conditions is met:

    a. Ownership is transferred from lessor to lessee.

    b. The lessee can buy the property at the end of the lease for less than market value.

    c. The lease's term is at least 75% of the asset's life.

    d. The lease payments have a present value of at least 90% of the asset's initial value. The discount rate is the lower of the rate used in the lease or the lessee's rate on equivalent new debt.

3. The lease payment is tax deductible by the lessee if the following conditions are met:

    a. The lease's term is less than 80% of the asset's remaining useful life

    b. The asset's estimated residual value must be at least 20% of its initial value.

c. The lessee has no right to buy the asset at a price set at the start of the lease.

d. The lessee does not pay any part of the price of the asset.

e. The asset cannot be limited use property.

4. The valuation of a lease is done by both the lessor and the lessee.

a. The lessor can evaluate the lease decision as a capital budgeting project.

1. The net investment is the following:

> *Net Purchase Price*
> *+ After-tax maintenance costs*
> *- After tax lease payment at time zero.*

2. The net benefits are:

> *After tax lease payments*
> *- After tax maintenance costs*
> *+ Depreciation tax savings*
> *+ After tax residual value*

3. The *discount rate* is the investor's opportunity cost, that is, the return on the next best alternative investment for the lessor.

4. The same decision rules apply here as for any capital budgeting project: Accept if the NPV is positive, reject if the NPV is negative.

b. The lessee calculates the *net advantage to leasing* (NAL) by calculating the cost of owning versus the cost of leasing:

1. The cost of owning is calculated in the same fashion as was done for the evaluation by the lessor. The only differences are that the lessee must use its own tax rate and its own after tax cost of debt.

2. The cost of leasing is calculated as the present value of the after tax lease payments, discounted at the after tax cost of new debt.
3. The net advantage to leasing is defined as:

$$NAL = Present\ value\ of\ cost\ of\ owning$$
$$- present\ value\ of\ cost\ of\ leasing \qquad (9.7)$$

C. Private Placement
 1. A *private placement* of securities, typically bonds, is a direct sale of the securities to the ultimate investor by the issuer. While the process may involve an intermediary such as an investment bank, the intermediary acts solely as a broker in the transaction.
 2. A private placement typically has the following features:
   a. By definition, it is not a market issue, therefore it is not subject to SEC registration.
   b. The interest rate is higher than comparable market issues, and is usually a fixed rate.
   c. There is more flexibility in the setting of terms than in a standard market issue. Despite the flexibility, the covenants in a private placement tend to be more restrictive.
   d. Maturities tend to be between three and fifteen years.
   e. The usual size is between $10 and $100 million.
D. Venture Capital
 1. *Venture capital* is a very risky, very active form of long term investment. A group of managers raises a pool of funds from investors, and then seeks out small, risky, but potentially extremely profitable firms in which to invest. A fund may evaluate hundreds of potential investments, but actually select only a few.
 2. The venture capitalists not only provide long term capital to the firms, but in many cases involve themselves directly in the management of the firms after the investment.

APPENDIX 9A: OPTION VALUATION

I. OPTIONS

A. A *call option* is a contract that gives the buyer the right to buy (sell, if it is a put option) an asset on or before a given date at a set price, after which date it becomes worthless.

B. There exist a large number of exchange traded options, stocks, currencies, bonds, and other financial instruments. As noted in the text, convertible securities contain option-like features, which can be valued in a manner similar to exchange traded options. Similarly, a warrant can be viewed as a long term option.

II. OPTION PRICING MODEL

A. *Black-Scholes Option Pricing Model*

1. The *Black-Scholes option pricing model* is the most common model for valuing options. The value of a European call (i.e., one that can be exercised only at expiration on a stock that pays no dividends) is given by the following:

$$V = P[N(d_1)] - Xe^{-rt}[N(d_2)] \qquad (9.8)$$

$$d_1 = \frac{Ln\left(\frac{P}{X}\right) + \left[r + \left(\frac{\sigma^2}{2}\right)\right]t}{\sigma\sqrt{t}} \qquad (9.9)$$

$$d_2 = d_1 - \sigma\sqrt{t} \qquad (9.10)$$

where:

V = value of the call option;

P = current price of the underlying stock;

$N[d_i)]$ = cumulative normal distribution for value d_i;

X = exercise price of the option;

e = base of the natural logarithm;

r = risk-free rate;

t = time to expiration of the option;

σ^2 = instantaneous variance of the stock's return.

2. As can be seen from the above equations, the value of a call option is a function of the current market price, the exercise price, the time to expiration, the risk free rate of interest, and the variability of returns on the underlying asset.

3. In general, a call option is more valuable with a longer time to expiration, more volatility in the underlying asset's return, a higher risk free rate, and a greater difference between the current price and the exercise price.

B. For a more detailed discussion of options and their pricing, please see Reilly, *Investment Analysis and Portfolio Management*, 4th edition, Chapter 20. (Fort Worth: Dryden Press, 1994).

CHAPTER 10
SHORT TERM
FINANCIAL MANAGEMENT

I. GENERAL CONSIDERATIONS
A. Nature of Cash and Liquidity
  1. _Cash_ is the most basic financial necessity of a business on a day-to-day basis. Virtually all payments a company makes must be in cash: payments for supplies, taxes, interest, and so on.
  2. _Liquidity_ is defined as the ability to convert an asset quickly into cash at a price very close to its current market price.
  2. Therefore, cash is by definition the most liquid asset. It also has the lowest explicit return, zero. The cash manager's problem is, therefore, to keep enough cash on hand to make the necessary payments, but not so much that earnings are reduced.
B. Working Capital
  1. _Working capital_ is the total amount of current assets a firm has.
  2. _Net working capital_ is the difference between a firm's current assets and current liabilities.
  3. _Working capital policy_ can be classified according to current asset and current liability management.
    a. A _conservative current asset policy_ is one that holds a large amount of current assets for liquidity. An _aggressive current asset policy_ holds smaller amounts of current assets in order to increase profitability.
    b. A _conservative current liability policy_ minimizes the amount of short term liabilities to reduce interest cost fluctuations and funding availability risk. Similarly, an _aggressive current liability policy_ holds larger amounts of short term liabilities to reduce interest costs.

c. A *conservative working capital policy* would therefore hold larger amounts of short term assets and smaller amounts of short term liabilities. An *aggressive working capital management policy* would hold smaller amounts of current assets and larger amounts of short term liabilities.

II. CASH AND MARKETABLE SECURITIES
A. Cash Balances
1. *Cash balances* consist of coin and paper money, and non-interest bearing demand deposits at depository institutions. Cash is held for two basic reasons:
   a. a transactions motive, to cover expected expenses;
   b. a precautionary motive, to cover unanticipated expenses.

A third motive, the speculative motive, was offered by Keynes. This is no longer relevant because of the close interest bearing cash substitutes now available to firms.

2. The *optimal cash balance* can be estimated using one of several techniques:
   a. The *EOQ*, or *Baumol*, model, which is given as:

$$C^* = \sqrt{\frac{2*F*T}{k}} \tag{10.1}$$

where:
   C*= optimal cash balance;
   F = fixed cost of obtaining cash;
   T = total amount of cash needed during the period;
   k = opportunity cost of holding cash.

   b. The *Miller-Orr model* takes into account the variability of cash flows. Mathematically, the model is composed of two equations:

$$z = \sqrt[3]{\frac{4b\sigma^2}{4i}} \qquad\qquad (10.2)$$

and

$$h = 3z \qquad\qquad (10.3)$$

where:
  z = the return point, that is, amount of cash placed into the cash account after cash balances reach zero;
  b = fixed cost associated with a security transaction;
  σ^2 = variance of daily net cash flows;
  i = daily interest rate, that is, the opportunity cost of holding cash;
  h = the upper limit on cash balances, the point at which an amount $h - z$ is transferred into securities.

B. Investments as Cash Substitutes
  1. Investment in securities as cash substitutes should be guided by the following considerations:
    a. Safety of principal, or default risk;
    b. Interest rate risk;
    c. Liquidity risk;
    d. Inflation risk;
    e. Yield.
  2. The above considerations tend to rule out longer term securities such as stocks and bonds as viable cash substitutes.
C. Types of Money Market Securities
  1. *Treasury bills* are short term direct obligations of the U.S. Treasury. These are the safest and typically carry the lowest yield.
  2. *Certificates of deposit* are issued by banks and other depository institutions.
  3. *Eurodollars* are dollar denominated deposits in a bank outside the U.S.

4. A *repurchase agreement* is a contract in which one party agrees to sell securities to the other and then buy them back at an agreed upon date, at a price set in the contract.

5. *Commercial paper* is a short term promissory note issued by corporations.

6. A *banker's acceptance* is a form of short term bank financing, in which the bank accepts the responsibility of paying a time draft drawn against it, making that draft a negotiable, or retradable, instrument. A *time draft* is an order to the bank to pay a specific amount of money at a definite time in the future.

7. A *money market mutual fund* is an investment pool that invests in short term, money market instruments such as the ones mentioned above.

D. Discount Rate Mathematics

1. Several of the money market instruments (Treasury bills, commercial paper, and bankers acceptances) are quoted on a discount rate basis. Prices and equivalent interest bearing yields are calculated in the following fashion.

2. The *discount* D from face value for a discount security is calculated as:

$$D = F * r_d * \frac{\#d}{360} \qquad (10.4)$$

where:
  D = dollar discount;
  F = face value of the security;
  r_d = the discount rate;
  #d = number of days to maturity.

The *price* P is therefore:

$$P = F - D \qquad (10.5)$$

The *discount rate* can be converted to an *equivalent simple interest rate*:

$$R = \frac{365 * r_d}{360 - r_d * (\#d)} \qquad (10.6)$$

The equivalent simple interest rate can also be found from the price and the discount:

$$R = \frac{D}{F - D} * \frac{365}{\#d} \qquad (10.7)$$

NOTE: This formula is strictly correct only for an instrument that has less than 182 days to maturity. For longer term securities, please see Marcia Stigum, *Money Market Calculations: Yields, Break-evens and Arbitrage*, Chapter 4 (Homewood, IL.: Dow Jones-Irwin, 1981).

EXAMPLE: Find the dollar discount, the price, and the equivalent yield for a $1,000,000 face value Treasury bill that has 90 days to maturity and a discount rate of 5%.

SOLUTION: Using equation 10.4, we have:

$$D = \$1,000,000 * .05 * \frac{90}{360}$$
$$= \$25,000$$

The price P is then:

$$P = \$1,000,000 - \$25,000$$
$$= \$975,000$$

Using equation 10.6, we find the equivalent yield:

$$R = \frac{365*.05}{360-.05*90}$$
$$= \frac{18.25}{355.50}$$
$$= .0513 \text{ or } 5.13\%$$

III. CREDIT MANAGEMENT AND ACCOUNTS RECEIVABLE

A. *Credit policy* refers to the terms and procedures under which a firm is willing to sell its goods on credit. The basic elements of credit policy are:

  1. Determination of creditworthiness. This is done through a financial evaluation of the potential borrower. This will involve the "Five C's of Credit" (please see below) and ratio analysis (please see Chapter 11.)

  2. Terms, which typically include the following:

    a. Credit limits;

    b. Due date;

    c. Discount, if any, for early payment;

    d. Discount payment date.

  3. Collection procedures.

  4. Procedures for handling bad debt.

B. The Five C's of Credit

  1. *Character* refers to the willingness of the borrower to repay the loan. Evidence of character can be found in past credit repayments, willingness to cooperate with the lender, and so forth.

  2. *Capacity* refers to the ability of the borrower to generate the means of repaying the loan.

  3. *Capital* refers to the net worth of the borrower and his/her ability to repay the loan if capacity for some reason is inadequate.

  4. *Collateral* refers to the assets pledged against the loan, or the security for the loan.

  5. *Conditions* refer to the covenants or terms placed in the loan to ensure performance on the part of the borrower.

C. Accounts Receivable
  1. An *account receivable* is an amount due from a customer
     for goods or services sold on credit.
  2. Accounts receivable represent an investment of cash.
     They are liquid only to the extent that they are collectible
     in a timely fashion are can be sold (i.e., factored).
  3. Accounts receivable can be increased or decreased by
     altering credit policy. For instance, reduction in credit
     standards can increase credit sales, but may also increase
     bad debt losses.

IV. INVENTORY MANAGEMENT
  A. Inventory
    1. *Inventory* is the stockpile of goods a firm has on hand
       either for production or for sale. There are three basic
       components to inventory:
       a. Raw materials
       b. Work in process
       c. Finished goods
  B. Economic Order Quantity Model
    1. The *economic order quantity* (EOQ) is the size of an
       order that minimizes the total inventory cost. For
       simplicity, the model assumes:
       a. Sales are uniform throughout the planning period;
       b. Parameters are fixed throughout the period;
       c. There is no uncertainty.
    2. Under these assumptions, the solution is:

$$EOQ = \sqrt{\frac{2FS}{CP}} \qquad (10.8)$$

where:
F = fixed cost to place an order;
S = annual sales;
C = carrying cost as a fraction of the sales price;
P = sales price.

3. Given the EOQ, you can find the number of orders:

$$\#Orders = \frac{S}{EOQ}$$ (10.9)

You can also find the total cost of the inventory:

$$TC = F*\#Orders + CP*\frac{EOQ}{2}$$ (10.10)

EXAMPLE: Find the economic order quantity if annual sales are expected to be 4,000 units, the fixed order cost is $4, the carrying cost is 10% of the sale price, and the sales price is $2.
SOLUTION: Using equation 10.8, we have:

$$EOQ = \sqrt{\frac{2*4*4,000}{.1*2}}$$
$$= \sqrt{\frac{16,000}{.1}}$$
$$= \sqrt{160,000} = 400$$

4. The *lead time* is the number of days it takes to receive an order. The *reorder point* is the number of units of inventory that will be sold during the lead time, leaving zero units on the shelf as the new order comes in. Mathematically, it is average daily sales times the lead time.
5. A *safety stock* is an additional number of units of inventory held to allow for uncertainty, such as in demand, or in arrival of shipments.

C. Just-In-Time Inventory Management
   1. *Just-In-Time* (JIT) inventory management is an arrangement made by a company with its suppliers to receive goods as needed for production

2. Managed properly, JIT reduces the inventory on hand and thus reduces inventory financing costs.
3. The risk in JIT is that there is a breakdown in the delivery system, causing disruptions in the production process.

V. SHORT TERM LIABILITY MANAGEMENT
A. Trade Credit

1. A major source of short term credit is *trade credit*, in which a supplier sells its goods to a customer for credit. This generates an account receivable for the supplier (see above) and an account payable for the customer.
2. The cost of credit to the customer, or the *cost of foregoing a discount*, is the interest cost of not taking advantage of the discount price. In effect, it is the extension of credit to the customer for the remaining term of the credit. The cost can be found by the following:

$$Cost = \frac{Discount(\%)}{100 - Discount(\%)} * \frac{365}{Final\,Date - Discount\,Date}$$

$$(10.11)$$

EXAMPLE: Find the cost of foregoing a 2% discount payable in 15 days, and paying on the final due date 45 days from sale (i.e., 2/15, net 45).
SOLUTION: From equation 10.11, we have:

$$Cost = \frac{2}{100 - 2} * \frac{365}{45 - 15}$$
$$= .0204 * 12.1667$$
$$= .2483 \text{ or } 24.83\%$$

Thus it would be cheaper to take out a bank loan at any interest rate less than 24.83% in order to pay on the discount due date.

B. Bank Loans
  1. A second major source of short term credit is *bank lending*. There are several types of short term bank loans:
     a. A *single payment*, or *"bullet" loan,* in which all principal and interest are paid on the maturity date.
     b. A *line of credit*, in which a borrower is given the right to withdraw the funds as needed, and to repay on or before a set date.
     c. A *revolving line of credit*, in which the borrower can use and pay back the funds several times over the term of the loan. This is similar to a credit card.
  2. The typical terms of bank loans include the following:
     a. The *interest rate* is the price paid for the use of the funds. The rate may be based on:
        1. The *prime rate*, which is currently the benchmark rate for loans of high quality.
        2. *LIBOR*, the *London Interbank Offered Rate*. This is a market rate based on Eurodollar rates in London.
        3. *Fed Funds*, the rate on overnight purchases and sales of excess reserve between banks.
        NOTE: The prime rate should not be defined as the lowest rate a bank offers its best customers. The practice of below prime lending has made this definition legally risky.
     b. A *compensating balance* is a part of the loan that is held as deposit at the lending bank. This obviously reduces the funds available to the borrower who still pays interest on the entire loan amount.
     c. *Fees* of various sorts are also charged. A *commitment fee* is charged if the loan agreement obligates the bank to provide funds at some future date at the option of the borrower. A *usage fee* (more precisely, a non-usage fee) is charged on the percentage of the loan that is not used during the period of a loan agreement.
     d. *Collateral* may be required. The collateral may have nothing to do directly with the loan (e.g., marketable

securities the firm owns), or it may be directly linked to the purpose of the loan. This latter is sometimes called *asset based lending*, and consists of accounts receivable loans and inventory loans.

e. *Covenants* will restrict the activities of the borrower. Typical covenants include minimum net worth requirements, minimum liquidity requirements, restrictions on additional borrowing, and the like.

3. The true cost of bank loans depends on the method used to compute interest:

a. Simple interest is computed by charging interest only on the original principal. The effective cost is thus the simple rate of interest.

b. Compound interest utilizes the equation for the effective annual rate (EAR), equation 1.18:

$$EAR = \left(1 + \frac{r}{q}\right)^q - 1.0 \qquad (10.12)$$

c. *Discount interest* is computed by subtracting the interest from the face amount of the loan. If the loan is for one year, the effective rate is given by:

$$EAR = \frac{Interest}{Face\ Value - Interest} \qquad (10.13)$$

More generally, it is given by:

$$EAR = \frac{r}{1 - r} \qquad (10.14)$$

where r is the nominal annual discount rate in decimal form.

d. *Interest with compensating balances* is similar to the case of discount interest. The effective rate for a one year loan is:

$$EAR = \frac{Interest}{Face\,Value - Compensating\,Balance} \qquad (10.15)$$

More generally the effective annual rate is given by:

$$EAR = \frac{r}{1-c} \qquad (10.16)$$

where c is the compensating balance requirement expressed as a decimal.

e. Add-on interest computes the interest on the face amount of the loan for the entire contract length. This interest is then added back to the original principal. The total amount is then divided by the number of payments to be made. The formula is:

$$R = \frac{2*\#\,annual\,payments*Interest}{(Total\,\#\,of\,payments + 1)*principal} \qquad (10.17)$$

EXAMPLE: Find the effective cost of a $1,000 loan under the following situations:
a. r = 10% and is paid back in two semi-annual payments;
b. a 10% discount rate;
c. a 10 annual rate with a 15% compensating balance requirement.
d. an add-on loan with 12 monthly payments and a nominal rate of 10%.
SOLUTION:
a. Using equation 10.12:

$$R = \left(1 + \frac{.10}{2}\right)^2 - 1$$
$$= (1.05)^2 - 1$$
$$= .1025 \text{ or } 10.25\%$$

b. Using equation 10.14:

$$R = \frac{10\%}{1-.10}$$
$$= 11.11\%$$

c. Using equation 10.16:

$$R = \frac{10\%}{1-.15}$$
$$= 11.76\%$$

d. Interest is $100, the total number of payments and the number of annual payments are 12, and principal is $1,000. Using equation 10.17:

$$R = \frac{2*12*100}{(12+1)*1,000}$$
$$= \frac{2,400}{13,000}$$
$$= .1846 \ or \ 18.46\%$$

C. Commercial Paper
  1. *Commercial paper* is a short term open market instrument issued by firms to raise cash. It is typically unsecured, sold on a discount basis, and has an initial maturity of less than 270 days.
  2. Access to the commercial paper market is restricted to larger companies with excellent credit ratings, or firms with backup lines of credit from a commercial bank.

CHAPTER 11
FINANCIAL ANALYSIS
AND PLANNING

I. PURPOSES OF ANALYSIS AND PLANNING
  A. Purposes of Financial Analysis
    1. To evaluate the past performance of the firm, in order to identify the firm's strong points and, more importantly, its weak points.
    2. To provide the basis for proper planning for the future of the firm.
  B. Purposes of Financial Planning
    1. To set goals for financial performance.
    2. To estimate the size and timing of future financial resource needs, both short and long term in nature.

NOTE: Perhaps nowhere else is the true nature of Finance so evident as in planning. Finance by its very nature is forward looking. A financial manager is constantly making decisions that affect the future course of the firm.

II. FINANCIAL STATEMENTS
  A. Balance Sheet
    1. The *Balance Sheet* is a record at a point in time of a firm's assets, liabilities, and net worth.
    2. Items are generally reported on the balance sheet at historical cost.
  B. Income Statement
    1. The *Income Statement* is a record of revenues, costs, and expenses for a specified period of time (e.g., a quarter, a year).
    2. Items are generally reported on the income statement on an accrual basis, that is, when revenue is earned or expenses incurred, not when they are received or paid.

C. Statement of Cash Flows
  1. The *Statement of Cash Flows* is the third of the financial statements a firm must produce. It records the comings and goings of cash, as opposed to the previous two statements, which record items on an accrual basis.
  2. The Statement of Cash Flows has three main sections:
    a. *Cash Flows from Operating Activities* include all the activities of the firm that are related to income generation. This includes income, expenses, and changes in working capital items.
    b. *Cash Flows from Investing Activities* include those resulting from the purchase or sale of real (physical) assets or long term financial assets that are not considered cash equivalent (e.g., preferred stock held as an investment).
    c. *Cash Flows from Financing Activities* involve the raising of funds from investors (stockholders and creditors) and the returns to these groups.
  3. There are two allowable ways to compute the statement of cash flows:
    a. The *direct method*;
    b. The *indirect method.*
  4. In addition to the Statement of Cash Flows, there are other definitions of cash flows that are useful.
    a. The most *general definition of cash flow* is:

$$Cash\ Flow\ =\ Net\ Income\ +\ Non\text{-}Cash\ Charges$$

(11.1)

    This definition is useful in capital budgeting, in which benefits include changes in depreciation expense.
    b. *Free cash flow* (FCF) is defined as cash generated from operations, less capital expenditures needed to maintain current productive capacity, and less dividend payments. Free cash flow is an indicator of the firm's ability to grow from internally generated sources.

III. RATIOS
  A. Ratio Analysis
   1. *Ratio analysis* is a technique of financial analysis in which certain relative values are calculated, and then are compared to the firm's previous results as well as to the firm's industry and competitors.
   2. There are several notes of caution in the use of ratios:
      a. Ratios are easy to calculate, but not necessarily easy to evaluate. The job of the analyst is to interpret the numbers correctly.
      b. By definition, ratios involve two numbers, a numerator and a denominator. Ratios that are out of the ordinary can be that way because either of these is too large or too small.
      c. Ratios are relative values, not absolute. The analyst must also keep in mind the size of the numbers involved.
      d. Ratios are sensitive to the particular accounting procedures used by the firm.
      e. Ratios, in and of themselves, say very little. It is necessary to compare the ratios to some standard, be it the industry, the firm itself over time, or preferably a combination of the two.
  B. Liquidity Ratios
   1. The *current ratio* is the ratio of current assets to current liabilities:

$$CR = \frac{Current\ Assets}{Current\ Liabilities} \qquad (11.2)$$

   2. The *quick ratio* is the ratio of current asset less inventories to current liabilities:

$$QR = \frac{Current\ Assets - Inventory}{Current\ Liabilities} \qquad (11.3)$$

C. Activity Ratios

  1. The *total asset turnover ratio* is the ratio of sales to total net assets:

$$TAT = \frac{Sales}{Net\ Assets} \qquad (11.4)$$

  NOTE: As a general rule, whenever the ratio involves an income statement item and a balance sheet item, one should average the balance sheet item over the relevant time period. This will reduce distortions caused by large changes in the balance sheet item.

  2. The *fixed asset turnover ratio* is the ratio of sales to net fixed assets:

$$FAT = \frac{Sales}{Net\ Fixed\ Assets} \qquad (11.5)$$

  3. The *inventory turnover ratio* is the ratio of sales to inventory:

$$ITR = \frac{Sales}{Average\ Inventory} \qquad (11.6)$$

  Alternatively, it can be defined as the ratio of cost of goods sold (COGS) to inventory:

$$ITR = \frac{COGS}{Average\ Inventory} \qquad (11.7)$$

  The second definition is preferred because inventory is valued at cost, while sales include a profit margin as well as cost. In practice, it is normal to use the first (i.e., sales) definition.

4. The *receivables turnover* (RT) is the ratio of sales to accounts receivable:

$$RT = \frac{Sales}{Accounts\ Receivable} \qquad (11.8)$$

5. The *average collection period* (ACP) is average number of days it takes to collect a receivable:

$$ACP = \frac{Accounts\ Receivable}{\left(Sales/365\right)} \qquad (11.9)$$

NOTE: There is no uniformity in the finance profession in the number of days, 360, 365, or actual days of operation, used in this equation. In actual cases, consult the industry practice.

NOTE: A handy way to remember the turnover ratios is to realize in all cases (but one) the numerator is sales, and the denominator is in the name of the ratio.

D. Leverage Ratios

1. *Leverage ratios* based on balance sheet items indicate the relative amounts of debt and equity used in funding a company. If you use total amounts of assets, liabilities, and equity, then all the various ratios contain the same information. This is due to the balance sheet identity TA = L + NW. A couple of the more common ones are:

a. The debt ratio (DR):

$$DR = \frac{Debt}{Total\ Assets} \qquad (11.10)$$

b. The equity multiplier (EM):

$$EM = \frac{Assets}{Equity} \qquad (11.11)$$

2. The *interest coverage ratio* is the number of times periodic interest payments can be made from EBIT:

$$ICR = \frac{EBIT}{Interest} \qquad (11.12)$$

3. The *fixed charge coverage ratio* is the number of times a firm could pay all fixed charges, typically interest and leasing, out of the income available to make such payments:

$$FCR = \frac{EBIT + Lease\ Payments}{Interest + Lease\ Payments} \qquad (11.13)$$

E. Profitability Ratios
   1. The *gross profit margin* measures the profitability of sales after deducting the cost of goods sold:

$$GPM = \frac{Sales\ Revenue - Cost\ of\ Goods\ Sold}{Sales\ Revenue} \qquad (11.14)$$

   2. The *net profit margin* is the ratio of net income to sales:

$$NPM = \frac{Net\ Income}{Sales\ Revenue} \qquad (11.15)$$

   3. The *return on assets* is the ratio of net income to total net assets:

$$ROA = \frac{Net\ Income}{Total\ Assets} \qquad (11.16)$$

   4. The *return on equity* is the ratio of net income to equity :

$$ROE = \frac{Net\ Income}{Equity} \qquad (11.17)$$

F. Market Value Ratios
   1. The *Price-Earnings ratio* (P/E) is the firm's current
     market price per share divided by its most current
     annualized earnings per share:

$$P\!/\!_E = \frac{price\ per\ share}{earnings\ per\ share} \tag{11.18}$$

   2. The *Market-to-Book ratio* (M/B) is the firm's market
     value (price per share times number of shares
     outstanding) divided by its book value:

$$M\!/\!_B = \frac{Market\ Value}{Book\ Value} \tag{11.19}$$

   3. In general, the higher these are, the better. However, a
     P/E that is well above the average could indicate a great
     deal of speculative interest in the stock. This interest
     could disappear with even slightly disappointing news.
G. The method of analysis known as *DuPont Analysis* permits
   a decomposition of ROE into several components. This
   decomposition can be expressed in one of several ways:

$$ROE = ROA * EM \tag{11.20}$$

$$ROE = NPM * TAT * EM \tag{11.21}$$

$$\frac{Net\ Income}{Equity} = \frac{Net\ Income}{Sales} * \frac{Sales}{Total\ Assets} * \frac{Total\ Assets}{Equity} \tag{11.22}$$

EXAMPLE: Given the following balance sheet and income
statement, calculate the ratios given above and perform the
DuPont analysis for the return on equity.

ASSETS		LIABILITIES	
CASH	2,000	ACCT PAY	4,000
ACCT REC	8,000	NOTE PAY	6,000
INVENTORY	10,000		
TOTAL CURR.		TOTAL CURR.	
ASSETS	20,000	LIAB.	10,000
		LONG TERM	
		DEBT	10,000
FIXED ASSETS	20,000	NET WORTH	20,000
TOTAL ASSETS	40,000	T.L. & N.W.	40,000

SALES	80,000
- COGS	60,000
- G&A	12,000
EBIT	8,000
- INTEREST	1,600
EBT	6,400
- TAX (@40%)	2,560
NET INCOME	3,840

SOLUTION:
Current ratio:

$$CR = \frac{20,000}{10,000} = \underline{2.0}$$

Quick ratio:

$$QR = \frac{10,000}{10,000} = \underline{1.0}$$

Total asset turnover ratio:

$$TAT = \frac{80,000}{40,000} = \underline{2.0}$$

Fixed asset turnover ratio:

$$FAT = \frac{80,000}{20,000} = \underline{4.0}$$

Inventory turnover ratio, using cost of goods sold:

$$ITR = \frac{60,000}{10,000} = \underline{6.0}$$

Receivables turnover ratio:

$$RT = \frac{80,000}{8,000} = \underline{10.0}$$

Average collection period:

$$ACP = \frac{8,000}{80,000 \Big/ 365} = \underline{36.5 \; days}$$

Debt ratio:

$$DR = \frac{20,000}{40,000} = \underline{.5 \; or \; 50\%}$$

Equity multiplier:

$$EM = \frac{40,000}{20,000} = \underline{2.0}$$

Interest coverage ratio:

$$ICR = \frac{8,000}{1,600} = \underline{5.0}$$

The fixed charge coverage ratio is the same as the interest coverage ratio because there are no lease payments.

Gross profit margin:

$$GPM = \frac{80,000 - 60,000}{80,000} = .75 \ or \ \underline{75\%}$$

Net profit margin:

$$NPM = \frac{3,840}{80,000} = .048 \ or \ \underline{4.8\%}$$

Return on assets:

$$ROA = \frac{3,840}{40,000} = .096 \ or \ \underline{9.6\%}$$

Return on equity:

$$ROE = \frac{3,840}{20,000} = .192 \ or \ \underline{19.2\%}$$

This last result can be obtained through DuPont analysis using ratios derived above:

$$ROE = NPM * TAT * EM$$
$$= 4.8\% * 2.0 * 2.0 = 19.2\%$$

G. Trend and Industry Comparisons
   1. In order to evaluate the firm's performance, it is necessary to compare the ratios to some standard. The two usual standards are the firm's own past values and the industry's averages.

2. Using the firm's past ratio values allows the analyst to identify any patterns in performance over time. For instance, in the case of the firm in the example above, the return on equity, while apparently high, may actually be lower than previous years. It is the analyst's job to find out why that may be the case.

3. Comparing the firm's ratios to industry averages also allows the analyst to identify unusual values. Refer again to the example above. The current and quick ratios appear to be in line with the conventional standards of 2 and 1, respectively. But it may be that the industry averages are 2.5 and 1.5. The firm in the example would therefore have less liquidity on the balance sheet than the average firm in the industry.

4. The above examples suggest a few more cautions in using ratio analysis:
   a. The analyst needs to know the circumstances of the firm and the industry at a given point in time. For instance, is the economy in a recession or expansion?
   b. In using industry averages, remember that averages can be affected by abnormally large or small values. Percentiles may be better to use than averages.

IV. FORECASTING FUNDS NEEDS
A. Cash Budgeting
1. *Cash budgeting* is the process of forecasting cash receipts and disbursements, in order to plan for possible borrowing to cover cash needs, or to plan for the investing of temporary cash surpluses.
2. The general process is as follows:
   a. Develop a sales forecast. This is the most important and most difficult step, because many others follow directly from it.
   b. Develop the production plan based on the sales forecast, and on beginning and ending inventory.
   c. Derive the costs of production.

d. Determine when cash receipts will be received.

e. Determine when cash payments for production and overhead costs will be due.

f. Estimate other cash receipts (e.g., investment income, etc.) and other cash expenditures (e.g., interest payments, dividend payments, taxes, etc.)

g. Find the total cash receipts and cash expenditures, and take the difference.

h. Having set a minimum desired cash balance, determine whether the cash balance is above or below that amount.

i. If the forecasted balance is below the minimum, plan for borrowings; if it is above, plan for temporary investments.

NOTE: Do not confuse expenses that appear on the income statement with cash items. For instance, depreciation is for many firms a major expense, but it is not a cash item. Therefore, while it appears on the income statement, it does not show up on the cash budget.

B. Additional Funds Needed

1. A second, and more approximate, method is the *additional funds needed* (AFN). This is the difference between the total cash funds needed to support the projected increase in sales and the sum of spontaneously generated funds and internally generated funds:

$$AFN = \frac{A}{S}(\Delta S) - \frac{L}{S}(\Delta S) - S(NPM)(1-d) \qquad (11.23)$$

where:

AFN = additional funds needed;

A = assets proportionately tied to sales;

L = liabilities proportionately tied to sales;

S = the *new* level of sales;

ΔS = the *increase* in sales;

NPM = net profit margin;

d = dividend payout ratio.

2. This method assumes that certain categories of assets and liabilities change automatically with a change in sales. These are typically cash, accounts receivable, inventories, and accounts payable. Other categories, such as fixed assets, can also be tied to sales. For instance, if the firm has no slack capacity in its operations, an increase in sales would force an increase in fixed assets as well.

EXAMPLE: Calculate the additional funds needed by a firm that currently has sales of $10,000,000 and is expecting an increase of $1,000,000. The firm's spontaneously generated assets are 75% of sales, while spontaneously generated liabilities are 25%. The net profit margin is 5%, and the firm pays out 60% of earnings in dividends.

SOLUTION: Using equation 11.23, we have:

$$AFN = .75*1,000,000 - .25*1,000,000$$
$$- 11,000,000*.05*(1-.6)$$
$$= 750,000 - 250,000 - 220,000$$
$$= 280,000$$

C. Regression Analysis
  1. *Regression analysis* is a statistical technique that is used to estimate relationships between variables.
  2. Linear least squares regression estimates a straight line relationship for a set of data:

$$Y_i = a + b*X_i + \varepsilon_i \qquad (11.24)$$

where:
Y_i = dependent variable, or the one to be explained;
b = regression coefficient to be estimated.
X_i = explanatory variable;
ε_i = error term.

The technique minimizes the sum of the squared error terms between the actual and forecasted values of Y. This results, for a simple regression in one explanatory variable, in the following formula for the estimate of b:

$$b = \frac{n * \sum_{i}^{n} Y_i * X_i - \sum_{i}^{n} Y_i * \sum_{i}^{n} X_i}{n \sum_{i}^{n} X_i^2 - \left(\sum_{i}^{n} X_i\right)^2} \qquad (11.25)$$

where n is the number of observations.
The constant a is estimated by:

$$a = \overline{Y} - b * \overline{X} \qquad (11.26)$$

3. The details of statistical estimation are beyond the scope of this book. A couple of points in the use of regression can be made here:

   a. In using regression to forecast, the analyst is making the assumption that the relationship between the dependent and explanatory variable(s) will remain the same. In an industry that is rapidly changing, this assumption is not valid, and regression will give poor forecasts.

   b. Just because there is a good statistical relationship between two variables in a regression, it does not mean that there is a causal relationship. It is the analyst's job to specify the relationship properly before estimation.

TABLES

TABLES

TABLE A.1: FUTURE VALUE OF $1
TABLE A.2: PRESENT VALUE OF $1
TABLE A.3: FUTURE VALUE OF $1 PER PERIOD
TABLE A.4: PRESENT VALUE OF $1 PER PERIOD
TABLE A.5: DEPRECIATION SCHEDULES
TABLE A.6: LIST OF FORMULAS
TABLE A.7: LIST OF SYMBOLS
TABLE A.8: LIST OF TEXTBOOKS

Table A.1 Future Value of $1 at the End of N Periods

$$FVIF(r,N) = (1+r)^N$$

Period	1%	2%	3%	4%	5%	6%	7%	8%	9%	10%
1	1.0100	1.0200	1.0300	1.0400	1.0500	1.0600	1.0700	1.0800	1.0900	1.1000
2	1.0201	1.0404	1.0609	1.0816	1.1025	1.1236	1.1449	1.1664	1.1881	1.2100
3	1.0303	1.0612	1.0927	1.1249	1.1576	1.1910	1.2250	1.2597	1.2950	1.3310
4	1.0406	1.0824	1.1255	1.1699	1.2155	1.2625	1.3108	1.3605	1.4116	1.4641
5	1.0510	1.1041	1.1593	1.2167	1.2763	1.3382	1.4026	1.4693	1.5386	1.6105
6	1.0615	1.1262	1.1941	1.2653	1.3401	1.4185	1.5007	1.5869	1.6771	1.7716
7	1.0721	1.1487	1.2299	1.3159	1.4071	1.5036	1.6058	1.7138	1.8280	1.9487
8	1.0829	1.1717	1.2668	1.3686	1.4775	1.5938	1.7182	1.8509	1.9926	2.1436
9	1.0937	1.1951	1.3048	1.4233	1.5513	1.6895	1.8385	1.9990	2.1719	2.3579
10	1.1046	1.2190	1.3439	1.4802	1.6289	1.7908	1.9672	2.1589	2.3674	2.5937
11	1.1157	1.2434	1.3842	1.5395	1.7103	1.8983	2.1049	2.3316	2.5804	2.8531
12	1.1268	1.2682	1.4258	1.6010	1.7959	2.0122	2.2522	2.5182	2.8127	3.1384
13	1.1381	1.2936	1.4685	1.6651	1.8856	2.1329	2.4098	2.7196	3.0658	3.4523
14	1.1495	1.3195	1.5126	1.7317	1.9799	2.2609	2.5785	2.9372	3.3417	3.7975
15	1.1610	1.3459	1.5580	1.8009	2.0789	2.3966	2.7590	3.1722	3.6425	4.1772
16	1.1726	1.3728	1.6047	1.8730	2.1829	2.5404	2.9522	3.4259	3.9703	4.5950
17	1.1843	1.4002	1.6528	1.9479	2.2920	2.6928	3.1588	3.7000	4.3276	5.0545
18	1.1961	1.4282	1.7024	2.0258	2.4066	2.8543	3.3799	3.9960	4.7171	5.5599
19	1.2081	1.4568	1.7535	2.1068	2.5270	3.0256	3.6165	4.3157	5.1417	6.1159
20	1.2202	1.4859	1.8061	2.1911	2.6533	3.2071	3.8697	4.6610	5.6044	6.7275
25	1.2824	1.6406	2.0938	2.6658	3.3864	4.2919	5.4274	6.8485	8.6231	10.8347
30	1.3478	1.8114	2.4273	3.2434	4.3219	5.7435	7.6123	10.0627	13.2677	17.4494
40	1.4889	2.2080	3.2620	4.8010	7.0400	10.2857	14.9745	21.7245	31.4094	45.2593
50	1.6446	2.6916	4.3839	7.1067	11.4674	18.4202	29.4570	46.9016	74.3575	117.3909

133

Table A.1 Future Value of $1 at the End of N Periods

$$FVIF(r,N) = (1+r)^N$$

Period	11%	12%	13%	14%	15%	16%	17%	18%	19%	20%
1	1.1100	1.1200	1.1300	1.1400	1.1500	1.1600	1.1700	1.1800	1.1900	1.2000
2	1.2321	1.2544	1.2769	1.2996	1.3225	1.3456	1.3689	1.3924	1.4161	1.4400
3	1.3676	1.4049	1.4429	1.4815	1.5209	1.5609	1.6016	1.6430	1.6852	1.7280
4	1.5181	1.5735	1.6305	1.6890	1.7490	1.8106	1.8739	1.9388	2.0053	2.0736
5	1.6851	1.7623	1.8424	1.9254	2.0114	2.1003	2.1924	2.2878	2.3864	2.4883
6	1.8704	1.9738	2.0820	2.1950	2.3131	2.4364	2.5652	2.6996	2.8398	2.9860
7	2.0762	2.2107	2.3526	2.5023	2.6600	2.8262	3.0012	3.1855	3.3793	3.5832
8	2.3045	2.4760	2.6584	2.8526	3.0590	3.2784	3.5115	3.7589	4.0214	4.2998
9	2.5580	2.7731	3.0040	3.2519	3.5179	3.8030	4.1084	4.4355	4.7854	5.1598
10	2.8394	3.1058	3.3946	3.7072	4.0456	4.4114	4.8068	5.2338	5.6947	6.1917
11	3.1518	3.4785	3.8359	4.2262	4.6524	5.1173	5.6240	6.1759	6.7767	7.4301
12	3.4985	3.8960	4.3345	4.8179	5.3503	5.9360	6.5801	7.2876	8.0642	8.9161
13	3.8833	4.3635	4.8980	5.4924	6.1528	6.8858	7.6987	8.5994	9.5964	10.6993
14	4.3104	4.8871	5.5348	6.2613	7.0757	7.9875	9.0075	10.1472	11.4198	12.8392
15	4.7846	5.4736	6.2543	7.1379	8.1371	9.2655	10.5387	11.9737	13.5895	15.4070
16	5.3109	6.1304	7.0673	8.1372	9.3576	10.7480	12.3303	14.1290	16.1715	18.4884
17	5.8951	6.8660	7.9861	9.2765	10.7613	12.4677	14.4265	16.6722	19.2441	22.1861
18	6.5436	7.6900	9.0243	10.5752	12.3755	14.4625	16.8790	19.6733	22.9005	26.6233
19	7.2633	8.6128	10.1974	12.0557	14.2318	16.7765	19.7484	23.2144	27.2516	31.9480
20	8.0623	9.6463	11.5231	13.7435	16.3665	19.4608	23.1056	27.3930	32.4294	38.3376
25	13.5855	17.0001	21.2305	26.4619	32.9190	40.8742	50.6578	62.6686	77.3881	95.3962
30	22.8923	29.9599	39.1159	50.9502	66.2118	85.8499	111.0647	143.3706	184.6753	237.3763
40	65.0009	93.0510	132.7816	188.8835	267.8635	378.7212	533.8687	750.3783	1051.668	1469.772
50	184.5648	289.0022	450.7359	700.2330	1083.657	1670.704	2566.215	3927.357	5988.914	9100.438

Table A.2 Present Value of $1 Due at the End of N Periods

$$PVIF(r,N) = 1/(1+r)^N$$

Period	1%	2%	3%	4%	5%	6%	7%	8%	9%	10%
1	0.9901	0.9804	0.9709	0.9615	0.9524	0.9434	0.9346	0.9259	0.9174	0.9091
2	0.9803	0.9612	0.9426	0.9246	0.9070	0.8900	0.8734	0.8573	0.8417	0.8264
3	0.9706	0.9423	0.9151	0.8890	0.8638	0.8396	0.8163	0.7938	0.7722	0.7513
4	0.9610	0.9238	0.8885	0.8548	0.8227	0.7921	0.7629	0.7350	0.7084	0.6830
5	0.9515	0.9057	0.8626	0.8219	0.7835	0.7473	0.7130	0.6806	0.6499	0.6209
6	0.9420	0.8880	0.8375	0.7903	0.7462	0.7050	0.6663	0.6302	0.5963	0.5645
7	0.9327	0.8706	0.8131	0.7599	0.7107	0.6651	0.6227	0.5835	0.5470	0.5132
8	0.9235	0.8535	0.7894	0.7307	0.6768	0.6274	0.5820	0.5403	0.5019	0.4665
9	0.9143	0.8368	0.7664	0.7026	0.6446	0.5919	0.5439	0.5002	0.4604	0.4241
10	0.9053	0.8203	0.7441	0.6756	0.6139	0.5584	0.5083	0.4632	0.4224	0.3855
11	0.8963	0.8043	0.7224	0.6496	0.5847	0.5268	0.4751	0.4289	0.3875	0.3505
12	0.8874	0.7885	0.7014	0.6246	0.5568	0.4970	0.4440	0.3971	0.3555	0.3186
13	0.8787	0.7730	0.6810	0.6006	0.5303	0.4688	0.4150	0.3677	0.3262	0.2897
14	0.8700	0.7579	0.6611	0.5775	0.5051	0.4423	0.3878	0.3405	0.2992	0.2633
15	0.8613	0.7430	0.6419	0.5553	0.4810	0.4173	0.3624	0.3152	0.2745	0.2394
16	0.8528	0.7284	0.6232	0.5339	0.4581	0.3936	0.3387	0.2919	0.2519	0.2176
17	0.8444	0.7142	0.6050	0.5134	0.4363	0.3714	0.3166	0.2703	0.2311	0.1978
18	0.8360	0.7002	0.5874	0.4936	0.4155	0.3503	0.2959	0.2502	0.2120	0.1799
19	0.8277	0.6864	0.5703	0.4746	0.3957	0.3305	0.2765	0.2317	0.1945	0.1635
20	0.8195	0.6730	0.5537	0.4564	0.3769	0.3118	0.2584	0.2145	0.1784	0.1486
25	0.7798	0.6095	0.4776	0.3751	0.2953	0.2330	0.1842	0.1460	0.1160	0.0923
30	0.7419	0.5521	0.4120	0.3083	0.2314	0.1741	0.1314	0.0994	0.0754	0.0573
40	0.6717	0.4529	0.3066	0.2083	0.1420	0.0972	0.0668	0.0460	0.0318	0.0221
50	0.6080	0.3715	0.2281	0.1407	0.0872	0.0543	0.0339	0.0213	0.0134	0.0085

Table A.2 Present Value of $1 Due at the End of N Periods

$$PVIF(r,N) = 1/(1+r)^N$$

Period	11%	12%	13%	14%	15%	16%	17%	18%	19%	20%
1	0.9009	0.8929	0.8850	0.8772	0.8696	0.8621	0.8547	0.8475	0.8403	0.8333
2	0.8116	0.7972	0.7831	0.7695	0.7561	0.7432	0.7305	0.7182	0.7062	0.6944
3	0.7312	0.7118	0.6931	0.6750	0.6575	0.6407	0.6244	0.6086	0.5934	0.5787
4	0.6587	0.6355	0.6133	0.5921	0.5718	0.5523	0.5337	0.5158	0.4987	0.4823
5	0.5935	0.5674	0.5428	0.5194	0.4972	0.4761	0.4561	0.4371	0.4190	0.4019
6	0.5346	0.5066	0.4803	0.4556	0.4323	0.4104	0.3898	0.3704	0.3521	0.3349
7	0.4817	0.4523	0.4251	0.3996	0.3759	0.3538	0.3332	0.3139	0.2959	0.2791
8	0.4339	0.4039	0.3762	0.3506	0.3269	0.3050	0.2848	0.2660	0.2487	0.2326
9	0.3909	0.3606	0.3329	0.3075	0.2843	0.2630	0.2434	0.2255	0.2090	0.1938
10	0.3522	0.3220	0.2946	0.2697	0.2472	0.2267	0.2080	0.1911	0.1756	0.1615
11	0.3173	0.2875	0.2607	0.2366	0.2149	0.1954	0.1778	0.1619	0.1476	0.1346
12	0.2858	0.2567	0.2307	0.2076	0.1869	0.1685	0.1520	0.1372	0.1240	0.1122
13	0.2575	0.2292	0.2042	0.1821	0.1625	0.1452	0.1299	0.1163	0.1042	0.0935
14	0.2320	0.2046	0.1807	0.1597	0.1413	0.1252	0.1110	0.0985	0.0876	0.0779
15	0.2090	0.1827	0.1599	0.1401	0.1229	0.1079	0.0949	0.0835	0.0736	0.0649
16	0.1883	0.1631	0.1415	0.1229	0.1069	0.0930	0.0811	0.0708	0.0618	0.0541
17	0.1696	0.1456	0.1252	0.1078	0.0929	0.0802	0.0693	0.0600	0.0520	0.0451
18	0.1528	0.1300	0.1108	0.0946	0.0808	0.0691	0.0592	0.0508	0.0437	0.0376
19	0.1377	0.1161	0.0981	0.0829	0.0703	0.0596	0.0506	0.0431	0.0367	0.0313
20	0.1240	0.1037	0.0868	0.0728	0.0611	0.0514	0.0433	0.0365	0.0308	0.0261
25	0.0736	0.0588	0.0471	0.0378	0.0304	0.0245	0.0197	0.0160	0.0129	0.0105
30	0.0437	0.0334	0.0256	0.0196	0.0151	0.0116	0.0090	0.0070	0.0054	0.0042
40	0.0154	0.0107	0.0075	0.0053	0.0037	0.0026	0.0019	0.0013	0.0010	0.0007
50	0.0054	0.0035	0.0022	0.0014	0.0009	0.0006	0.0004	0.0003	0.0002	0.0001

Table A.3 Future Value of $1 per Period at the End of N Periods

$$FVIFA(r,N) = [(1+r)^N - 1]/r$$

Period	1%	2%	3%	4%	5%	6%	7%	8%	9%	10%
1	1.0000	1.0000	1.0000	1.0000	1.0000	1.0000	1.0000	1.0000	1.0000	1.0000
2	2.0100	2.0200	2.0300	2.0400	2.0500	2.0600	2.0700	2.0800	2.0900	2.1000
3	3.0301	3.0604	3.0909	3.1216	3.1525	3.1836	3.2149	3.2464	3.2781	3.3100
4	4.0604	4.1216	4.1836	4.2465	4.3101	4.3746	4.4399	4.5061	4.5731	4.6410
5	5.1010	5.2040	5.3091	5.4163	5.5256	5.6371	5.7507	5.8666	5.9847	6.1051
6	6.1520	6.3081	6.4684	6.6330	6.8019	6.9753	7.1533	7.3359	7.5233	7.7156
7	7.2135	7.4343	7.6625	7.8983	8.1420	8.3938	8.6540	8.9228	9.2004	9.4872
8	8.2857	8.5830	8.8923	9.2142	9.5491	9.8975	10.2598	10.6366	11.0285	11.4359
9	9.3685	9.7546	10.1591	10.5828	11.0266	11.4913	11.9780	12.4876	13.0210	13.5795
10	10.4622	10.9497	11.4639	12.0061	12.5779	13.1808	13.8164	14.4866	15.1929	15.9374
11	11.5668	12.1687	12.8078	13.4864	14.2068	14.9716	15.7836	16.6455	17.5603	18.5312
12	12.6825	13.4121	14.1920	15.0258	15.9171	16.8699	17.8885	18.9771	20.1407	21.3843
13	13.8093	14.6803	15.6178	16.6268	17.7130	18.8821	20.1406	21.4953	22.9534	24.5227
14	14.9474	15.9739	17.0863	18.2919	19.5986	21.0151	22.5505	24.2149	26.0192	27.9750
15	16.0969	17.2934	18.5989	20.0236	21.5786	23.2760	25.1290	27.1521	29.3609	31.7725
16	17.2579	18.6393	20.1569	21.8245	23.6575	25.6725	27.8881	30.3243	33.0034	35.9497
17	18.4304	20.0121	21.7616	23.6975	25.8404	28.2129	30.8402	33.7502	36.9737	40.5447
18	19.6147	21.4123	23.4144	25.6454	28.1324	30.9057	33.9990	37.4502	41.3013	45.5992
19	20.8109	22.8406	25.1169	27.6712	30.5390	33.7600	37.3790	41.4463	46.0185	51.1591
20	22.0190	24.2974	26.8704	29.7781	33.0660	36.7856	40.9955	45.7620	51.1601	57.2750
25	28.2432	32.0303	36.4593	41.6459	47.7271	54.8645	63.2490	73.1059	84.7009	98.3471
30	34.7849	40.5681	47.5754	56.0849	66.4388	79.0582	94.4608	113.2832	136.3075	164.4940
40	48.8864	60.4020	75.4013	95.0255	120.7998	154.7620	199.6351	259.0565	337.8824	442.5926
50	64.4632	84.5794	112.7969	152.6671	209.3480	290.3359	406.5289	573.7702	815.0836	1163.909

Table A.3 Future Value of $1 per Period at the End of N Periods

$$FVIFA(r,N) = [(1+r)^N - 1]/r$$

Period	11%	12%	13%	14%	15%	16%	17%	18%	19%	20%
1	1.0000	1.0000	1.0000	1.0000	1.0000	1.0000	1.0000	1.0000	1.0000	1.0000
2	2.1100	2.1200	2.1300	2.1400	2.1500	2.1600	2.1700	2.1800	2.1900	2.2000
3	3.3421	3.3744	3.4069	3.4396	3.4725	3.5056	3.5389	3.5724	3.6061	3.6400
4	4.7097	4.7793	4.8498	4.9211	4.9934	5.0665	5.1405	5.2154	5.2913	5.3680
5	6.2278	6.3528	6.4803	6.6101	6.7424	6.8771	7.0144	7.1542	7.2966	7.4416
6	7.9129	8.1152	8.3227	8.5355	8.7537	8.9775	9.2068	9.4420	9.6830	9.9299
7	9.7833	10.0890	10.4047	10.7305	11.0668	11.4139	11.7720	12.1415	12.5227	12.9159
8	11.8594	12.2997	12.7573	13.2328	13.7268	14.2401	14.7733	15.3270	15.9020	16.4991
9	14.1640	14.7757	15.4157	16.0853	16.7858	17.5185	18.2847	19.0859	19.9234	20.7989
10	16.7220	17.5487	18.4197	19.3373	20.3037	21.3215	22.3931	23.5213	24.7089	25.9587
11	19.5614	20.6546	21.8143	23.0445	24.3493	25.7329	27.1999	28.7551	30.4035	32.1504
12	22.7132	24.1331	25.6502	27.2707	29.0017	30.8502	32.8239	34.9311	37.1802	39.5805
13	26.2116	28.0291	29.9847	32.0887	34.3519	36.7862	39.4040	42.2187	45.2445	48.4966
14	30.0949	32.3926	34.8827	37.5811	40.5047	43.6720	47.1027	50.8180	54.8409	59.1959
15	34.4054	37.2797	40.4175	43.8424	47.5804	51.6595	56.1101	60.9653	66.2607	72.0351
16	39.1899	42.7533	46.6717	50.9804	55.7175	60.9250	66.6488	72.9390	79.8502	87.4421
17	44.5008	48.8837	53.7391	59.1176	65.0751	71.6730	78.9792	87.0680	96.0218	105.9306
18	50.3959	55.7497	61.7251	68.3941	75.8364	84.1407	93.4056	103.7403	115.2659	128.1167
19	56.9395	63.4397	70.7494	78.9692	88.2118	98.6032	110.2846	123.4135	138.1664	154.7400
20	64.2028	72.0524	80.9468	91.0249	102.4436	115.3797	130.0329	146.6280	165.4180	186.6880
25	114.4133	133.3339	155.6196	181.8708	212.7930	249.2140	292.1049	342.6035	402.0425	471.9811
30	199.0209	241.3327	293.1992	356.7868	434.7451	530.3117	647.4391	790.9480	966.7122	1181.882
40	581.8261	767.0914	1013.704	1342.025	1779.090	2360.757	3134.522	4163.213	5529.829	7343.858
50	1668.771	2400.018	3459.507	4994.521	7217.716	10435.65	15089.50	21813.09	31515.34	45497.19

138

Table A.4 Present Value of $1 per Period for N Periods

$$PVIFA(r,N) = [1/r] - 1/[r(1+r)^N]$$

Period	1%	2%	3%	4%	5%	6%	7%	8%	9%	10%
1	0.9901	0.9804	0.9709	0.9615	0.9524	0.9434	0.9346	0.9259	0.9174	0.9091
2	1.9704	1.9416	1.9135	1.8861	1.8594	1.8334	1.8080	1.7833	1.7591	1.7355
3	2.9410	2.8839	2.8286	2.7751	2.7232	2.6730	2.6243	2.5771	2.5313	2.4869
4	3.9020	3.8077	3.7171	3.6299	3.5460	3.4651	3.3872	3.3121	3.2397	3.1699
5	4.8534	4.7135	4.5797	4.4518	4.3295	4.2124	4.1002	3.9927	3.8897	3.7908
6	5.7955	5.6014	5.4172	5.2421	5.0757	4.9173	4.7665	4.6229	4.4859	4.3553
7	6.7282	6.4720	6.2303	6.0021	5.7864	5.5824	5.3893	5.2064	5.0330	4.8684
8	7.6517	7.3255	7.0197	6.7327	6.4632	6.2098	5.9713	5.7466	5.5348	5.3349
9	8.5660	8.1622	7.7861	7.4353	7.1078	6.8017	6.5152	6.2469	5.9952	5.7590
10	9.4713	8.9826	8.5302	8.1109	7.7217	7.3601	7.0236	6.7101	6.4177	6.1446
11	10.3676	9.7868	9.2526	8.7605	8.3064	7.8869	7.4987	7.1390	6.8052	6.4951
12	11.2551	10.5753	9.9540	9.3851	8.8633	8.3838	7.9427	7.5361	7.1607	6.8137
13	12.1337	11.3484	10.6350	9.9856	9.3936	8.8527	8.3577	7.9038	7.4869	7.1034
14	13.0037	12.1062	11.2961	10.5631	9.8986	9.2950	8.7455	8.2442	7.7862	7.3667
15	13.8651	12.8493	11.9379	11.1184	10.3797	9.7122	9.1079	8.5595	8.0607	7.6061
16	14.7179	13.5777	12.5611	11.6523	10.8378	10.1059	9.4466	8.8514	8.3126	7.8237
17	15.5623	14.2919	13.1661	12.1657	11.2741	10.4773	9.7632	9.1216	8.5436	8.0216
18	16.3983	14.9920	13.7535	12.6593	11.6896	10.8276	10.0591	9.3719	8.7556	8.2014
19	17.2260	15.6785	14.3238	13.1339	12.0853	11.1581	10.3356	9.6036	8.9501	8.3649
20	18.0456	16.3514	14.8775	13.5903	12.4622	11.4699	10.5940	9.8181	9.1285	8.5136
25	22.0232	19.5235	17.4131	15.6221	14.0939	12.7834	11.6536	10.6748	9.8226	9.0770
30	25.8077	22.3965	19.6004	17.2920	15.3725	13.7648	12.4090	11.2578	10.2737	9.4269
40	32.8347	27.3555	23.1148	19.7928	17.1591	15.0463	13.3317	11.9246	10.7574	9.7791
50	39.1961	31.4236	25.7298	21.4822	18.2559	15.7619	13.8007	12.2335	10.9617	9.9148

Table A.4 Present Value of $1 per Period for N Periods
$$PVIFA(r,N) = [1/r] - 1/[r(1+r)^N]$$

Period	11%	12%	13%	14%	15%	16%	17%	18%	19%	20%
1	0.9009	0.8929	0.8850	0.8772	0.8696	0.8621	0.8547	0.8475	0.8403	0.8333
2	1.7125	1.6901	1.6681	1.6467	1.6257	1.6052	1.5852	1.5656	1.5465	1.5278
3	2.4437	2.4018	2.3612	2.3216	2.2832	2.2459	2.2096	2.1743	2.1399	2.1065
4	3.1024	3.0373	2.9745	2.9137	2.8550	2.7982	2.7432	2.6901	2.6386	2.5887
5	3.6959	3.6048	3.5172	3.4331	3.3522	3.2743	3.1993	3.1272	3.0576	2.9906
6	4.2305	4.1114	3.9975	3.8887	3.7845	3.6847	3.5892	3.4976	3.4098	3.3255
7	4.7122	4.5638	4.4226	4.2883	4.1604	4.0386	3.9224	3.8115	3.7057	3.6046
8	5.1461	4.9676	4.7988	4.6389	4.4873	4.3436	4.2072	4.0776	3.9544	3.8372
9	5.5370	5.3282	5.1317	4.9464	4.7716	4.6065	4.4506	4.3030	4.1633	4.0310
10	5.8892	5.6502	5.4262	5.2161	5.0188	4.8332	4.6586	4.4941	4.3389	4.1925
11	6.2065	5.9377	5.6869	5.4527	5.2337	5.0286	4.8364	4.6560	4.4865	4.3271
12	6.4924	6.1944	5.9176	5.6603	5.4206	5.1971	4.9884	4.7932	4.6105	4.4392
13	6.7499	6.4235	6.1218	5.8424	5.5831	5.3423	5.1183	4.9095	4.7147	4.5327
14	6.9819	6.6282	6.3025	6.0021	5.7245	5.4675	5.2293	5.0081	4.8023	4.6106
15	7.1909	6.8109	6.4624	6.1422	5.8474	5.5755	5.3242	5.0916	4.8759	4.6755
16	7.3792	6.9740	6.6039	6.2651	5.9542	5.6685	5.4053	5.1624	4.9377	4.7296
17	7.5488	7.1196	6.7291	6.3729	6.0472	5.7487	5.4746	5.2223	4.9897	4.7746
18	7.7016	7.2497	6.8399	6.4674	6.1280	5.8178	5.5339	5.2732	5.0333	4.8122
19	7.8393	7.3658	6.9380	6.5504	6.1982	5.8775	5.5845	5.3162	5.0700	4.8435
20	7.9633	7.4694	7.0248	6.6231	6.2593	5.9288	5.6278	5.3527	5.1009	4.8696
25	8.4217	7.8431	7.3300	6.8729	6.4641	6.0971	5.7662	5.4669	5.1951	4.9476
30	8.6938	8.0552	7.4957	7.0027	6.5660	6.1772	5.8294	5.5168	5.2347	4.9789
40	8.9511	8.2438	7.6344	7.1050	6.6418	6.2335	5.8713	5.5482	5.2582	4.9966
50	9.0417	8.3045	7.6752	7.1327	6.6605	6.2463	5.8801	5.5541	5.2623	4.9995

TABLE A.5 Depreciation Schedules

CLASS YEAR	3 YEAR %	5 YEAR %	7 YEAR %	10 YEAR %	15 YEAR %	20 YEAR %
1	33.33	20.00	14.29	10.00	5.00	3.75
2	44.45	32.00	24.49	18.00	9.50	7.22
3	14.81	19.20	17.49	14.40	8.55	6.67
4	7.41	11.52	12.49	11.52	7.70	6.18
5		11.52	8.93	9.22	6.93	5.71
6		5.76	8.92	7.37	6.23	5.29
7			8.93	6.55	5.90	4.89
8			4.46	6.55	5.90	4.52
9				6.56	5.91	4.46
10				6.55	5.90	4.46
11				6.55	5.91	4.46
12				3.28	5.90	4.46
13					5.91	4.46
14					5.90	4.46
15					5.91	4.46
16					2.95	4.46
17						4.46
18						4.46
19						4.46
20						4.46
21						2.23

TABLE A.6
LIST OF FORMULAS

$$FV_N = PV_0 * (1+r)^N \qquad (1.1)$$

$$FV_N = PV_0 * FVIF(r, N) \qquad (1.2)$$

$$FVA_N = A * \frac{\left[(1+r)^N - 1\right]}{r} \qquad (1.3)$$

$$FVA_N = A * FVIFA(r, N) \qquad (1.4)$$

$$FVAD_N = A * \frac{\left[(1+r)^N - 1\right]}{r} * (1+r) \qquad (1.5)$$

$$FVAD_N = A * FVIFA(r, N) * (1+r) \qquad (1.6)$$

$$PV_0 = \frac{FV_N}{(1+r)^N} \qquad (1.7)$$

$$PV_0 = FV_N * PVIF(r, N) \qquad (1.8)$$

$$PVA_N = A * \frac{\left[1 - (1+r)^{-N}\right]}{r} \qquad (1.10)$$

$$PVA_0 = A * PVIFA(r, N) \qquad (1.11)$$

$$PVAD = A * \frac{\left[1 - (1+r)^{-N}\right]}{r} * (1+r) \qquad (1.12)$$

$$PVAD = A * PVIFA(r, N) * (1+r) \qquad (1.13)$$

$$PVP = \frac{A}{r} \qquad (1.14)$$

$$FV_N = PV_0 * \left(1 + \frac{r}{q}\right)^{N*q} \qquad (1.15)$$

$$FV_N = PV_0 * e^{r*N} \qquad (1.17)$$

$$EAR = \left(1 + \frac{r_{nom}}{q}\right)^{q} - 1.0 \qquad (1.18)$$

$$HPR = \frac{P_N - P_0}{P_0} + \frac{\sum_{t=1}^{N} CF_t}{P_0} \qquad (2.1)$$

$$\overline{R} = \frac{HPR_1 + HPR_2 + ... + HPR_N}{N} \qquad (2.4)$$

$$\overline{G} = \left[(1 + HPR_1)(1 + HPR_2)...(1 + HPR_N)\right]^{\frac{1}{N}} - 1 \qquad (2.6)$$

$$E(R) = R_1 * P(R_1) + R_2 * P(R_2) + ... + R_N * P(R_N) \qquad (2.8)$$

$$\sigma^2 = \frac{\left(R_1 - \overline{R}\right)^2 + \left(R_2 - \overline{R}\right)^2 + ... + \left(R_N - R\right)^2}{N - 1} \qquad (2.10)$$

$$\sigma = \sqrt{\sigma^2} \qquad (2.11)$$

$$\sigma^2 = \left[R_1 - E(R)\right]^2 * P(R_1) + \left[R_2 - E(R)\right]^2 * P(R_2) + ...$$
$$\qquad (2.13)$$
$$+ \left[R_N - E(R)\right]^2 * P(R_N)$$

$$CV = \frac{\sigma}{\overline{R}} \tag{2.14}$$

$$E(R_P) = w_1 E(R_1) + w_2 E(R_2) + \ldots + w_N E(R_N) \tag{2.17}$$

$$\rho_{XY} = \frac{Cov_{XY}}{\sigma_X \sigma_Y} \tag{2.21}$$

$$\sigma_p^2 = w_1^2 \sigma_1^2 + w_2^2 \sigma_2^2 + \rho_{1,2} w_1 w_2 \sigma_1 \sigma_2 \tag{2.23}$$

$$E(R_p) = R_F + \sigma_p \left[\frac{E(R_M) - R_F}{\sigma_M} \right] \tag{2.26}$$

$$E(R_i) = R_F + \beta_i \left[E(R_M) - R_F \right] \tag{2.27}$$

$$\beta_i = \frac{Cov_{i,M}}{\sigma_M^2} \tag{2.28}$$

$$\beta_p = w_1 \beta_1 + w_2 \beta_2 + \ldots + w_N \beta_N \tag{2.33}$$

$$V_s = \sum_{t=1}^{N} \frac{CF_t}{(1+k)^t} = \frac{CF_1}{(1+k)} + \frac{CF_2}{(1+k)^2} + \ldots + \frac{CF_N}{(1+k)^N} \tag{3.1}$$

$$V_B = \sum_{t=1}^{N} \frac{I_t}{(1+k_b)^t} + M * \frac{1}{(1+k_b)^N} \tag{3.2}$$

$$AYTM = \frac{I_t + \dfrac{(M - P_0)}{N}}{\dfrac{P_0 + M}{2}} \tag{3.11}$$

$$AYTC = \frac{I_t + \dfrac{CP_c - P_0}{C}}{\dfrac{CP_c + P_0}{2}}$$

(3.13)

$$ARR = \left(\frac{TV_N}{PV_0}\right)^{\frac{1}{N}} - 1$$

(3.15)

$$V_P = \frac{D_P}{k_P}$$

(3.16)

$$V_E = \sum_{t=1}^{N} \frac{D_t}{(1+k_e)^t} + \frac{E(P_N)}{(1+k_e)^N}$$

(3.17)

$$V_E = \frac{D_1}{k_e - g} = \frac{D_0(1+g)}{k_e - g}$$

(3.18)

$$V_E = \sum_{t=1}^{N} \frac{D_t}{(1+k_e)^t} + \frac{D_{N+1}}{k_e - g}\left(\frac{1}{1+k_e}\right)^N$$

(3.19)

$$g = b * ROE$$

(3.20)

$$k_d = k_b(1 - T)$$

(4.1)

$$k_p = \frac{D_p}{P_p - F}$$

(4.2)

$$k_s = \frac{D_1}{P_0} + g$$

(4.4)

$$k_s = R_F + \beta[E(R_M) - R_F]$$

(4.5)

$$k_e = \frac{D_1}{P_e - F} + g \tag{4.6}$$

$$WACC = w_d k_b (1 - T) + w_p k_p + w_e k_e \tag{4.8}$$

$$Break\ Point = \frac{Amount\ Available\ from\ Source}{The\ Fraction\ of\ Capital\ the\ Source\ Represents} \tag{4.9}$$

$$Q_{BE} = \frac{F}{P - V} \tag{5.1}$$

$$DOL = \frac{\%\Delta EBIT}{\%\Delta SALES} = \frac{\dfrac{EBIT_2 - EBIT_1}{EBIT_1}}{\dfrac{SALES_2 - SALES_1}{SALES_1}} \tag{5.4}$$

$$DOL = \frac{Q(P - V)}{Q(P - V) - F} \tag{5.5}$$

$$DFL = \frac{\%\Delta EPS}{\%\Delta EBIT} = \frac{\dfrac{EPS_2 - EPS_1}{EPS_1}}{\dfrac{EBIT_2 - EBIT_1}{EBIT_1}} \tag{5.7}$$

$$DFL = \frac{EBIT}{EBIT - I} \tag{5.8}$$

$$DCL = \frac{\%\Delta EPS}{\%\Delta SALES} = \frac{\dfrac{EPS_2 - EPS_1}{EPS_1}}{\dfrac{SALES_2 - SALES_1}{SALES_1}} \tag{5.9}$$

$$DCL = \frac{Q(P-V)}{Q(P-V)-F-I} \qquad (5.10)$$

$$DCL = DOL * DFL \qquad (5.12)$$

$$\frac{(EBIT - I_1)(1-T)}{S_1} = \frac{(EBIT - I_2)(1-T)}{S_2} \qquad (5.13)$$

$$V_U = V_L \qquad (6.1)$$

$$k_{sL} = k_{sU} + (k_{sU} - k_d)\left(D\!\!\not{\;}_S\right) \qquad (6.3)$$

$$V_L = V_U + TD \qquad (6.4)$$

$$k_{sL} = k_{sU} + (k_{sU} - k_d)(1-T)\left(D\!\!\not{\;}_S\right) \qquad (6.6)$$

$$k_{sL} = k_{RF} + (k_M - k_{RF}) * \beta_U + (k_M - k_{RF}) * \beta_U * (1-T) * D\!\!\not{\;}_S \qquad (6.7)$$

$$\beta_L = \beta_U \left[1 + (1-T) * D\!\!\not{\;}_S\right] \qquad (6.8)$$

$$V_L = V_U + \left[1 - \frac{(1-T_C)(1-T_S)}{(1-T_D)}\right] D \qquad (6.9)$$

$$\Delta CF_t = \Delta NI_t + \Delta Dep_t \qquad (7.6)$$

$$NPV = \sum_{t=1}^{N} \frac{\Delta CF_t}{(1+k)^t} - NINV \qquad (7.8)$$

$$\sum_{t=1}^{N} \frac{\Delta CF_t}{(1+IRR)^t} - NINV = 0 \qquad (7.9)$$

$$MIRR = \left(\frac{TV_N}{NINV}\right)^{\frac{1}{N}} - 1 \qquad (7.11)$$

$$PI = \frac{\sum_{t=1}^{N}\frac{\Delta CF_t}{(1+k)^t}}{NINV} \qquad (7.12)$$

$$v_{on} = \frac{P_0 - P_s}{N+1} \qquad (9.1)$$

$$v_{ex} = \frac{P_0 - P_s}{N} \qquad (9.2)$$

$$V = P\left[N(d_1)\right] - Xe^{-rt}\left[N(d_2)\right] \qquad (9.8)$$

$$d_1 = \frac{Ln\left(\frac{P}{X}\right) + \left[r + \left(\frac{\sigma^2}{2}\right)\right]t}{\sigma\sqrt{t}} \qquad (9.9)$$

$$d_2 = d_1 - \sigma\sqrt{t} \qquad (9.10)$$

$$D = F * r_d * \frac{\#d}{360} \qquad (10.4)$$

$$P = F - D \qquad (10.5)$$

$$R = \frac{365 * r_d}{360 - r_d * (\#d)} \qquad (10.6)$$

$$EOQ = \sqrt{\frac{2FS}{CP}} \qquad (10.8)$$

$$Cost = \frac{Discount(\%)}{100 - Discount(\%)} * \frac{365}{Final\ Date - Discount\ Date} \quad (10.11)$$

$$EAR = \frac{r}{1-r} \quad (10.14)$$

$$EAR = \frac{r}{1-c} \quad (10.16)$$

$$R = \frac{2*\#\ annual\ payments*Interest}{(Total\ \#\ of\ payments + 1)*principal} \quad (10.17)$$

$$CR = \frac{Current\ Assets}{Current\ Liabilities} \quad (11.2)$$

$$QR = \frac{Current\ Assets - Inventory}{Current\ Liabilities} \quad (11.3)$$

$$TAT = \frac{Sales}{Net\ Assets} \quad (11.4)$$

$$FAT = \frac{Sales}{Net\ Fixed\ Assets} \quad (11.5)$$

$$ITR = \frac{Sales}{Average\ Inventory} \quad (11.6)$$

$$ACP = \frac{Accounts\ Reccivable}{\left(Sales/365\right)} \quad (11.9)$$

$$DR = \frac{Debt}{Total\ Assets} \quad (11.10)$$

$$EM = \frac{Assets}{Equity} \tag{11.11}$$

$$ICR = \frac{EBIT}{Interest} \tag{11.12}$$

$$FCR = \frac{EBIT + Lease\ Payments}{Interest + Lease\ Payments} \tag{11.13}$$

$$NPM = \frac{Net\ Income}{Sales\ Revenue} \tag{11.15}$$

$$ROA = \frac{Net\ Income}{Total\ Assets} \tag{11.16}$$

$$ROE = \frac{Net\ Income}{Equity} \tag{11.17}$$

$$ROE = NPM * TAT * EM \tag{11.21}$$

$$AFN = \frac{A}{S}(\Delta S) - \frac{L}{S}(\Delta S) - S(NPM)(1-d) \tag{11.23}$$

TABLE A.7
LIST OF SYMBOLS

A	- Annuity	DCL	- Degree of combined leverage
A	- Asset	DFL	- Degree of financial leverage
AFN	- Additional funds needed	DOL	- Degree of operating leverage
ARR	- Annual realized rate of return	E	- Expected value
ARR	- Accounting rate of return	$E(R_M)$	- Expected market return
AYTC	- Approximate yield to call	EAR	- Effective annual return
AYTM	- Approximate yield to maturity	EBIT	- Earnings before interest and taxes
b	- Retention rate	EOQ	- Economic order quantity
β	- Beta	EPS	- Earnings per share
C	- Years to call	F	- Face value
C	- Carrying cost of inventory, percent of price	F	- Fixed cost
		F	- Fixed ordering cost
c	- Percent compensating balance requirement	F	- Flotation cost, in dollars
CF	- Cash flow	f	- Flotation cost, in percent of issue price
COV	- Covariance		
CP	- Call price		
CV	- Coefficient of variation	FV	- Future value
		FVA	- Future value of an ordinary annuity
D	- Dollar discount		
D	- Dividend	FVAD	- Future value of an annuity due
D	- Market value of debt	$\overline{G}$	- Geometric average
d	- Dividend payout rate	g	- Growth rate
#d	- Number of days	HPR	- Holding period return

151

I	- Interest	q	- Number of compounding periods in a year
IRR	- Internal rate of return		
k	- Required return or cost of capital	R	- Return (actual)
		$\overline{R}$	- Arithmetic average
k_b	- Pre-tax cost of debt	R_F	- Risk-free rate
k_d	- After-tax cost of debt	r	- Interest rate
		r_d	- Discount rate
k_e	- Cost of equity, or cost of new common stock	ρ	- Correlation coefficient
		ROA	- Return on assets
k_p	- Cost of preferred stock	ROE	- Return on equity
		S	- Market value of equity
k_s	- Cost of retained earnings	S	- Sales
L	- Liability	σ	- Standard deviation
M	- Principal or maturity value	σ^2	- Variance
		T	- Tax rate
MIRR	- Modified internal rate of return	t	- Time
		TV	- Terminal value
N	- Number of years	V	- Value
NINV	- Net investment	V	- Variable cost
NPV	- Net present value	v	- Value of a right
P	- Price	w	- Weight
PI	- Profitability index	WACC	- Weighted average cost of capital
PV	- Present value		
PVA	- Present value of an ordinary annuity	X	- Exercise price
		YTC	- Yield to Call
PVAD	- Present value of an annuity due	YTM	- Yield to Maturity
PVP	- Present value of a perpetuity		
Q	- Quantity		
Q_{BE}	- Break-even quantity		

TABLE A.8
LIST OF TEXTBOOKS

The following is a list of current textbooks in financial management. In the charts that follow the list, each major topic is listed along with the relevant chapters in that text. The list is not intended to be exhaustive, but representative. Inclusion in or exclusion from the list should not be construed as my opinion on the quality or value of a particular text. The texts are alphabetical by first author and are identified in the tables the same way.

Stanley Block and Geoffrey Hirt, *Foundations of Financial Management*, 7th ed. (Irwin, 1994)

Richard Brealey, Stewart Myers, and Alan J. Marcus, *Fundamentals of Corporate Finance*, (McGraw-Hill, 1995)

Eugene Brigham, *Fundamentals of Financial Management*, 7th ed. (Dryden, 1995)

Philip Cooley, *Business Financial Management*, 3rd ed. (Dryden, 1994)

Bodil Dickerson, B.J. Campsey, and Eugene Brigham, *Introduction to Financial Management* , 3rd ed. (Dryden, 1991)

Douglas Emery and John Finnerty, *Principles of Finance*, (West, 1991)

Lawrence Gitman, *Principles of Managerial Finance*, 7th ed. (HarperCollins, 1994)

R. Charles Moyer, James McGuigan, and William Kretlow, *Contemporary Financial Management*, 6th ed. (West, 1995)

J William Petty, Arthur Keown, David Scott Jr., John Martin, *Basic Financial Management*, (Prentice Hall, 1993)

George E. Pinches, *Financial Management*, (HarperCollins, 1994)

Ramesh Rao, *Financial Managment*, 3rd ed. (South-Western, 1995)

Stephen Ross, Randolph Westerfield, and Bradford Jordan, *Fundamentals of Corporate Finance*, 3rd. ed. (Irwin , 1995)

James C. Van Horne and John M. Wachowicz, *Fundamentals of Financial Management,* 9th ed. (Prentice Hall, 1995)

J. Fred Weston, Scott Besley, and Eugene F Brigham, *Essentials of Managerial Finance*, 11th ed. (Dryden, 1996)

AUTHOR TOPIC	BLOCK HIRT	BREALEY ET AL.	BRIGHAM	COOLEY	DICKERSON ET AL.	EMERY FINNERTY	GITMAN
TIME VALUE	9	3	4	4	13	3	5
RISK & RETURN	13	9	5	5	12	7	6
VALUATION	10	4,5	7	6	16,17	6	7
COST OF CAPITAL	11	11	8	6	19	10	10
LEVERAGE	5	8	12	7	20	26	11
CAPITAL STRUCTURE	11(A)	15	12	7	20	15,16,19	11
CAPITAL BUDGETING	12,13	6,7,8	9,10,11	8,9,10	14,15	11,12,13	8,9

AUTHOR	BLOCK HIRT	BREALEY ET AL.	BRIGHAM	COOLEY	DICKERSON ET AL.	EMERY FINNERTY	GITMAN
TOPIC							
DIVIDEND POLICY	18	16	13	19	21	17,18	13
LONG TERM FINANCING	14,15,16,17	12,13,14	14,15,16	17,18,20	16,17,18	14,20,21	12,13,14
SHORT TERM MANAGEMENT	6,7,8	19,20,21	18,19,20	11,12,13,14	8,9,10,11	25,26	16,17,18
FINANCIAL ANALYSIS	3	2,17,18	2,3,17	15,16	5,6,7	24	15

AUTHOR TOPIC	MOYER, ET AL.	PETTY, ET AL.	PINCHES	RAO	ROSS, ET AL.	VAN HORNE	WESTON ET AL.
TIME VALUE	5	3	2	4	5	3	6
RISK & RETURN	6	4	4	5,6,7	10,11	5	5
VALUATION	7,8	5	3	13,14	6	4	7
COST OF CAPITAL	12	8	6	10	14	15,18	15
LEVERAGE	13,14	9	9	19	15	16	16
CAPITAL STRUCTURE	13,14	10	11,12	15	15	17,18	16
CAPITAL BUDGETING	9,10,11	6,7	7,8,9,10	8,9,10	7,8,9	13,14	13,14

AUTHOR TOPIC	MOYER, ET AL.	PETTY, ET AL.	PINCHES	RAO	ROSS, ET AL.	VAN HORNE	WESTON ET AL.
DIVIDEND POLICY	15	11	13	17	16	18	17
LONG TERM FINANCING	7,8,19,20	18,19,20,21	15,1617,18	12,13,14,18	12,13	19,20 21,22	18, 19, 20
SHORT TERM MANAGEMENT	16,17,18	14,15,16,17	19,20,21,22	21,22,23,	17,18,19	8,9, 10,11	8, 9, 10, 11,12
FINANCIAL ANALYSIS	4	12,13	24,25	20	3,4	6,7	3, 4

158

INDEX

161